Destructive
Creativity *of*

and the
East Asian Response

and the
East Asian Response

Destructive
Creativity *of*

and the
East Asian Response

Michael Heng Siam-Heng
Lim Tai Wei
East Asian Institute, National University of Singapore, Singapore

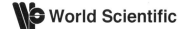

World Scientific

NEW JERSEY · LONDON · SINGAPORE · BEIJING · SHANGHAI · HONG KONG · TAIPEI · CHENNAI

Published by

World Scientific Publishing Co. Pte. Ltd.

5 Toh Tuck Link, Singapore 596224

USA office: 27 Warren Street, Suite 401-402, Hackensack, NJ 07601

UK office: 57 Shelton Street, Covent Garden, London WC2H 9HE

British Library Cataloguing-in-Publication Data
A catalogue record for this book is available from the British Library.

DESTRUCTIVE CREATIVITY OF WALL STREET AND THE EAST ASIAN RESPONSE

ISBN-13 978-981-4273-78-7
ISBN-10 981-4273-78-3

Typeset by Stallion Press
Email: enquiries@stallionpress.com

Printed in Singapore.

Preface

The ongoing financial crisis and economic recession are likely to go down in history as a defining feature of this decade. It is too rash to predict what the long term consequences are. But the short-term impacts are too clear and unfortunately for many either too painful or too unpleasant to forget.

The book you are reading is but one of several if not dozens that try to inform and analyze the crisis. It is intended for the general public. We have therefore avoided jargons and terms which are too technical. If we fail in our attempt, we are grateful if you could kindly write to us so as to assist us in our future book projects.

Before the advent of modernization, the term "innovation" had a bad press. Since then it has enjoyed accolade and is associated with something progressive, forward-looking and wealth creation. Joseph Schumpeter had given us the concept of "creative destruction". But innovation is a double-edged sword too, and this is told through the story of Frankenstein. It is displayed on the stage of history in the form of technologies and systems that may not have always benefitted human kind. It is to convey our ambivalent feelings about innovation that explains the first half of the title of this book.

Writing a book on an unfolding event has its excitement and difficulties. It is exciting because there is a stream of interesting terms and ideas in the mass media. It is difficult because we do not have the benefit of hindsight to reflect. At the same time, it is difficult to decide on a cut-off point. In that sense, this book is a work-in-progress, and hopefully we have the opportunity to return to finish the project.

We are aware that there will be detractors and we welcome comments. Indeed, colleagues and friends who have read some of the chapters are forthcoming in their views. In particular we would like to thank Dr. Sven Fischer, Professor Huang Jing and Mr. Lie Chen-Ie for pointing out the mistakes and ambiguities in the drafts. As authors of the final draft, we alone are responsible for weaknesses in the book. We hope you will join them in clarifying our thoughts and in helping us to write a better book in the future.

We would also like to thank Mr. Ho Kwon Ping for his kind permission to let us reproduce excerpts of his speech at the Singapore Venture Capital Association Gala Dinner on 30th September 2008.

Finally we would like to thank Ms. Lim Shujuan, the editor in charge of the project from our publisher World Scientific. Her skill and patience have made the work lighter by the kilograms.

Michael Heng Siam-Heng
Lim Tai Wei
30 January 2009

Contents

CHAPTER 1

Introduction

The United States of America has been hit by the collapses or near-collapses of Bear Stearns, Indy Mac, Lehman Brothers, Washington Mutual, Wachovia, Fannie Mae, Freddie Mac, the American Insurance Group and the Citigroup. To quote the US Secretary of Treasury of the Bush Administration, Henry M. Paulson, Jr., "Each of these failures would be tremendously consequential in its own right."[1]

To give us a sense of the magnitude and the gravity of the current bailout, here are some figures associated with the current financial situation. If we add up the sum of the funds committed so far by the US government, the figure is certainly mind-boggling. According to Jim Bianco of Bianco Research, it is bigger than the combined costs of the Marshall Plan, the Louisiana Purchase, the New Deal, the Korean War, the Vietnam War, NASA, the Moon Landing Program, Savings & Loans debacle and the invasion of Iraq. All these big-ticket items total $3.92 trillion, adjusted for inflation. With the Citigroup bailout added in, the current total cost exceeds $4.62 trillion. It is arguably the biggest injection of funds in American history. The only single event in US history of this magnitude is World War II. The original cost of World War II was $288 billion or $3.6 trillion when adjusted for inflation, which is still less than the $4.6 trillion we are talking about.[a,2]

The crisis has engulfed the world as the global economy slipped into recession. The economic data so far suggests that the recession will be deep and painful. There is general consensus that the world is facing the worst economic meltdown since the Great Depression. However, the world can avoid descending into depression if governments adopt the right measures.

No Two Financial Crises are the Same

In a strange way, financial crises bear certain similarities with earthquakes.[3] Long periods of calm are interrupted by short periods of violent tremors. During the calm period, pressure is slowly building up. A point is reached when disaster strikes. The tremors release the stress built up and after a while, calm returns. This cycle then repeats.

To understand how and why the credit system promotes economic growth, with its inevitability of boom and bust, let us begin with the calm period. The volatility is low, the system is stable and the profit outlook is good. Under the pressure to reward investors with more profits, corporations take on more risk. They assume more debts in order to increase their productive capacity. Banks are just too keen to lend. When times are good, they lower their guard. As stock prices climb, investors, having exhausted their funds, start to borrow to buy more stocks. Both corporations and investors take on more leveraging. The profits are so seductive when the going is good. The practice can become a habit for some time. This is a time of irrational exuberance when the bubble is building up.

---

[a] Unless otherwise stated, the $ sign in the book refers to US$

A point will come when the bubble bursts. Assets must be liquidated quickly to pay back the loan; money must be found to unwind the leveraging. In panic, investors rush for the door. Before long, we have a fire sale going on. Banks which cannot get their money back just go bankrupt. With the bleak business outlook, banks are very reluctant to lend to even viable businesses. We have a credit crunch, which aggravates the situation. To make the best out of the situation, management retrenches staff, persuades the rest to work harder without overtime pay, squeezes the suppliers and offers discounts to the buyers. If all these fail, the company goes bankrupt. Gloom overtakes euphoria and the economy slips into recession. The financial system reveals its fragility in its "full glory". Millions of innocent bystanders become the victims of greedy speculators. Their suffering provides rich material for social critics to hammer at the ills of capitalism. A global financial crisis suggests the possibility of some fundamental weakness of the international financial system, and sparks calls for redesigning the international financial architecture. But when the hurricane blows over, it carries away with it the honest anxiety. It is business again as usual, until the next turmoil. Are we going to see a replay of the story?

Financial crises share common features, yet their details differ. The Asian financial crisis took the form of currency crisis, degenerated into economic crisis and, in the case of Indonesia, ended up as political crisis. The dot-com bubble affected mainly the technological sector, and did not cause a panic in the banking and financial firms. The current turmoil is often described in the following terms: *credit crunch*, *banking crisis*, and *the worst since the Great Depression*. Expectedly, the financial industry is the worst affected, with bankruptcy, absorption, and the rest suffering sharp drops in stock prices.

What is this book about?

Banking and financial firms (BFFs) have a few crucial roles to play in economic activities, namely, as payment systems, in efficient allocation of financial resources, and in hedging risks associated with uncertainties.

Over the past several decades, the BFFs have undergone crucial changes as a result of the broader business and political environment. The global economy is more integrated and there is deregulation across a range of business activities. The application of advanced IT has enabled BFFs to take advantage of this environment to weave a tightly integrated network of financial systems.

Operating under a competitive free market environment, BFFs are under immense pressure to earn more profits. They resort to more and more financial instruments like derivatives and develop an appetite for risk taking, often with money entrusted to them for safe custody by their clients. Bankers are generously rewarded for the profits they make, while there is lax control of the risks undertaken by them. This encourages the well known behaviour of moral hazard. Under the watch of Alan Greenspan, the bankers had never had it so good. The financial service industry accounted for a large share of American total corporate profits. The share rose from 10% in the early 1980s to 40% at its peak in 2007, the profits in the past decades are in the order of trillions.[4]

The current round of financial crisis is extremely serious as a result of a convergence of a number of factors: huge current account deficits of the US, deregulation, loose monetary policy, and excessive liquidity, shoddy underwriting, abuse of derivatives, negligence of credit-rating agencies and lax government oversight. The subprime problem is but one of the many problems. Other problems are credit-card debt, student-loan debt, auto loans, commercial real estate loans, home-equity loans, corporate debt and loans that financed leveraged buyouts. The magnitude of the crisis inspires the economist Nouriel Roubini to observe: "We have a subprime financial system, not a subprime mortgage market." The scenario of the financial system falling like dominoes certainly gains currency as the crisis broadens and deepens.

The current crisis provides a valuable occasion for the world to re-examine the nature of the financial market. This book sets out to take a hard look at deregulation, derivatives, leveraging, remuneration systems, and rating agencies.

Our point of departure is that as custodians of depositors' or clients' money, BFFs should exercise due prudence in using that money to make more money. It does not mean that BFFs should take no risk at all. Commercial banks enjoy deposit guarantees by government and they often also function as important nodes in the payment systems. For these reasons, they should be regulated and not allowed to go into investment banking. Though investment banks have more leeway, it does not mean that they can operate in a totally unregulated manner. At the very least, they should abide by the principle that the risk taker should have the capacity to absorb the full risk without transmitting the risk to others. An analogy may be used: Formula One drivers are allowed to display their skills on special race circuits, but not on roads used by normal traffic.

While derivatives are useful financial instruments for those directly involved in the business, abuse of these has a toxic effect. This is especially so when BFFs assume risks that are beyond their capacity to bear. When they go bust, those who buy their products are left to suffer. It is not too far-fetched to compare derivatives to certain medical drugs. Used appropriately for patients who need them, the benefits are obvious. Abuse of them is harmful and can even be deadly.

BFFS should heed the warning of Peter Drucker that they should stop taking risky positions using their clients' money as a way of making profit. Rather they should innovate and find ways to add value to the clients. It may be added that BFFs must not harm the interests of society. In their earlier days, BFFs were very innovative and played a crucial role in promoting economic growth. They invented the letter of credit, check, insurance, stock exchange, credit card, etc. In the electronic business environment, they have the work cut out for them. The sad thing to note is that most of the financial innovations of electronic business are the works of non-BFFs.

Returning to the current financial crisis, there are clear signs that it is hitting the real economy, with recession a distinct reality rather than possibility. If managed well, the world may avoid a depression. The costs to tax payers are obviously immense, amounting to trillions. And like in the past financial crises, the worst hit are those workers who lose their jobs to pay for the sins of the "best and brightest bankers". Other countries also have to pay a heavy price. At the same time, the recent crisis has dealt a massive blow to the position of New York City as the premier world financial centre.

The bright side of the picture is that the world has gathered much experience in managing financial crises. Most important of all, the underlying real economy is not damaged in the way that it has been affected in history — by wars, political chaos, famine and other natural catastrophes.

Moreover, relatively speaking, the emerging economies especially China are not so severely affected by what is happening in the US. This book will look at why Asian economies have been less affected by the global financial crisis thus far and some like Japan have even managed to go on a buying spree of American financial institutions. Is corporate governance the main reason here? Or culture, management styles or even a state-led model? Did the Asian sovereign wealth funds help to be the last line of defence against the excesses of the crisis? All these commonly-cited features of the so-called Asian state-led model of development will be examined in this book. In this trend of thought, debates surrounding the hybrid Chinese model of capitalistic free marketplace and authoritarian political system will also be examined.

The crisis has also prompted some to turn to regulation as a panacea. Is Asian-style state-led models with its characteristic governmental intervention and host of regulation the defence mechanism that protected Asian economies from the crisis?

In the discussion of proposed solutions to the financial crisis, it is often pointed out that unilateralism is to be condemned, especially in the European case where non-coordination is often cited in comparison with the US's prompt and coordinated response in coming up with the $700 billion bailout package. In the spirit of coordination versus unilateralism, this book will examine

Asia's response. Is Asia yet another example of unilateral action towards the crisis or is the $80 billion Asian crisis fund the first instance of a coordinated East Asian response to the crisis. Would this truly underpin the creation of an East Asian regional order that would eventually lead to instruments like the Asian Monetary Fund or currency swaps leading to a full-blown convertible regional currency? Is the Asian way of quiet diplomacy also applicable to their management of the global financial crisis? Is the preferred channel of bilateralism an alternative or hindrance to the East Asian response? Can Northeast Asian powers truly reconcile with each other to create a regional order that would eventually have an impact on the global financial system?

Ultimately, is the much vaunted decoupling of Asian economies from the US proven by the financial crisis or to the contrary? Can East Asia create an insulated regional order or will this crisis prompt greater intra-regional coordination and a collective response in dealing with extra-regional state and non-state actors in the global economic and financial systems?

The crisis has revealed certain fundamental issues of the information economy. Financial services have been rightly seen as a good example of information economy. This book re-affirms the need for value adding, due regard for societal interest and that there is no free lunch.

Finally, to give our readers a flavour of views from the business world, we reproduce excerpts of a speech in the Appendix containing the reflections of Mr. Ho Kwon Ping, a trained economist who was once a journalist and who is a successful entrepreneur now.

PART ONE

Destructive Creativity of Wall Street

CHAPTER 2

Potted History of Banking and Finance

As a way of seeing how banking and finance have played a positive role in the past in promoting economic development, we first take a historical perspective to examine the emergence of modern banking and finance in Europe. The early history of banking in the West can be read as a story of the evolution of banks in the process of meeting the needs of modern commerce.

There was an interesting change in Europe in the early period of last millennium. Towns were gradually being transformed from bishops' seats of administration and fortified havens into vital centers of economic life.[1] They also began to play an important role in political development. When the kingship was powerful, a coherent political system was in effective operation. When it was weak, the kingdom would dissolve into a collection of petty principalities, free cities, and even city republics. Italy was perhaps the most extreme example of such disintegrated political arrangement. This change proved favorable for cities like Venice, Florence, and Genoa. In the early 13th century, they bloomed to become economic and cultural centres. The new social and economic milieu gave rise to new social behavior and ways of thinking.

Venice was a great commercial centre. Trade required the exchange of money. Banks in Europe began as money changers who specialized in assaying and valuing the coins used in the market centres. In fact, the word "bank" is derived from the Italian word *banco*, the small table or bench on which the banker kept his accounts of deposits and loans. It was in Venice that banking began to separate itself from the changing of money. They evolved to become deposit banks, acting as custodians of their clients' money. This transition proved to be very useful to bankers as traders gradually learned to trust the banks. With traders coming to accept book entry transfers as payment for their merchandise, banks acquired the role as payment intermediary between buyers and sellers. As long as the depositors could trust the banks, most of their money laid idle there. This interesting fact was soon discovered by the bankers. They realized that they could hold some reserves against deposits, and lend out the rest against some collateral or invest in promising business ventures. With this new business activity, they carried out additional roles as financial intermediary between savers and investors/borrowers, or become investors themselves.

While Venice was the Mediterranean commercial city par excellence, Florence was the cultural hub. Florence was the focus of the most intense and influential of cultural activities in Europe. From 1350 to 1450, more scholars, artists, scientists, architects and poets lived and worked in Italy than anywhere else in the Western world. Many of them came from other countries to participate in and contribute to that great unplanned historical phenomenon that later became known as the Renaissance. In the words of the historian John Roberts, "Europe went, as it were, to school there."[2]

The intellectual life in Italy at that time was fermenting and vigorous. Against this background of intellectual vitality, flourishing commerce brought with it a chain of institutional innovations. The Bill of Exchange appeared in the 13th century along with the first bankers. Limited liability was known in Florence in 1408, and marine insurance was available before that. Double-entry book-keeping was introduced to meet the needs of the merchants. By 1500, Italians had invented new credit instruments for the financing of international commerce. The Amsterdam stock exchange was established in early 17th century.[3] The 19th century saw the regular market being replaced by continuous trading, purchase by sample, the rise of shop keeping, and replacement of fairs by produce exchanges or bourses. In Europe, banks were established in centres of great foreign trade such as Venice, Amsterdam, Hamburg and Nuremberg. Merchant capital created markets, financed manufactures, floated the American colonial economies and launched banking and insurance.

Financial instruments of capitalism were invented in the course of turning the wheels of commerce. An extremely significant innovation was the principle and practice of limited liability. The practice of limiting the liability of passive partners made it easier for companies to attract investors to participate in new business ventures. It provided an efficient means for entrepreneurs to pool public financial resources by selling their shares on the stock exchange. It is an instrument for sharing risks and profits that proved crucial in the growth of capitalism. This has proved to be a very ingenious way to close the gap between demand and supply of capital in the service of risky and productive business projects through efficient and self-regulatory means.

Importance of Banks and Financial Companies

Earlier on, we have seen the evolution of banks from money-changers to financial intermediary between savers and borrowers. By doing so, banks and financial companies have become powerful and crucial institutions of contemporary economic life by providing liquidity to the economy. This has far-reaching societal consequences, in the forms of benefits and risks.

The benefits are well expressed by the economist Joseph Schumpeter: "The banker, therefore, is not so much primarily a middleman in the commodity 'purchasing power' as a producer of this commodity.... He stands between those who wish to form new combinations and the possessors of productive means. He is essentially a phenomenon of development, though only when no central authority directs the social process. He makes possible the carrying out of new combinations, authorises people, in the name of society as it were, to form them. He is the ephor of the exchange economy."[4]

The risks come in the form of turbulence in an economy which uses credit. The economist John Keynes points out that economic disturbances start in the sphere of money and finance and move to the real economy, rather than the other way around.[5]

Recently, some scholars even argue that what the actual and would-be economic leaders of the past five centuries have in common is the development of strong financial systems *before* they become economic leaders or contenders for economic leadership.[6]

The industry continued to display innovative spirit until the 1970s, though most of the innovations may not be as profound as the earlier times. For example, the two decades between 1950 and 1970 were productive and dynamic periods. First was the Eurodollar, an innovative product of the London bankers in response to the need of the Soviet Union. During the Cuban missile crisis in 1961–1962, the Russian State Bank was afraid that its foreign reserves parked in the US could be frozen. It wished to move the money to London but retain it in US dollars. Thus, a new financial product was born — a transnational currency denominated in US dollars but domiciled in London. Subsequently, the US administration wanted to impose tax on payments of bank interest to foreign depositors. Foreign deposits fled into the arms of London banks which offered them Eurobond.[7]

There was also institutional investment started by the General Motors fund, the first modern pension fund created in 1950. This was soon followed by many companies, setting off a boom in corporate pension funds. The new demand was met by new financial firms specializing in servicing the new institutional investors.[8]

Following the proliferation of multinational companies in the 1950s, banks and financial firms became multinational too. They operated in all major business capitals, in ways very similar to multinationals of other industries. For example, a British bank operating in Singapore would not only serve British MNCs operating in Singapore, it would also serve all other firms. It would do business with domestic Singapore firms and foreign firms just like any other bank under the supervision of the Singapore authorities. These big banks and financial firms have transformed into financial services institutions. They are in the business of managing and financing acquisitions, mergers and divestitures, financing equipment purchase or leasing worldwide, and financing global expansion of manufacturing and commercial companies.[9]

To the laymen, the most obvious innovation was the credit card, which appeared in the 1960s. It became an international "currency" and the most convenient form of payment for travellers. This novel service was a new life-line to commercial banks whose traditional business has been captured by the new financial services institutions.

Besides doing business closely associated with financing, the banking industry displayed great skill in using information technology. For example, the Bank of America was a pioneer in its use of computer technology in the 1950s to automate check processing.[10] Together with General Electric and the Stanford Research Institute, it is generally credited with inventing modern centralized bank operations, and introduced a number of financial transaction processing technologies such as automatic check processing, account numbers, magnetic ink character recognition and credit cards linked directly to individual bank accounts. Due to its clever and innovative use of these technologies, the bank had been able to significantly lower its costs and to become the world's largest bank in the early 1970s.

The financial industry played a positive role in another way. This sector as a whole was a big investor in computer technology. This has certainly boosted the growth of the computer industry even before the advent of the personal computers.

The Dawn of Deregulation

In the midst of innovative waves in the financial industry, something interesting happened. It was a trend towards financial deregulation. It turned out to be one of the defining characteristics of the economic landscape since the 1960s. With the petering out of innovations mentioned earlier, this new environment saw a new wave of innovation broadly known as financial engineering. We are also entering a period where we experience increasingly frequent and severe bouts of financial instability. Subsequent chapters shall explore the extent to which these fancy financial instruments may be implicated.

CHAPTER 3

In the Shadow of Depression?

In the midst of deepening crises in the world's major financial markets, some say we are hearing echoes of the Great Depression of the 1930s. The D-word has occurred with increasing frequency in the media. Even the previous US President George W. Bush commented at the G20 financial summit in November 2008 that it was conceivable that the US could suffer a depression worse than the Great Depression.

There is little doubt that the US and many other countries are in deep and painful recession. But Depression? Most likely not. There are several reasons why we should see the glass as half full — and not shattered — and focus our minds on relieving the pain inflicted by the recession.

Firstly, the post-World War II system of economic governance, in both the developed and developing world, is better equipped to deal with downturns than were the governments of the 1930s. John Maynard Keynes provided the theoretical tools for this system of governance. A policy instrument is counter-cyclical government spending to create demand during economic downturn by incurring budget deficits.

Another tool comes in the form of the central bank acting as lender of last resort. While working to stabilize the financial system, the central bank should lend freely, at a penalty rate, on good collateral. Companies that would be bankrupt in normal times should be left to disappear. The idea was worked out by Walter Bagehot, a British businessman and essayist, in his famous work *Lombard Street: a description of the money market.*[1]

Furthermore, the central bank's monetary policy to slash interest rates. A lower interest rate reduces the cost of borrowing in economic downturn. Moreover, it is read as the government's willingness to help turn the economy around. With oil and other commodities becoming cheaper in anticipation of lower demand, the danger of inflation recedes. This makes it easier for central banks to cut interest rates.

The second reason is that the banking and payment systems are still at work. Thanks to deposit guarantee, only 19 banks had failed by mid-November 2008.[2] The demise of Wall Street icons like Lehman Brothers is certainly shocking, but it is a far cry from the failure of 4,000 commercial banks in 1933.

The third reason for optimism has to do with the flow of credit. Unlike the dot-com bubble in the previous crisis, the key feature of the current one lies in the credit market. The flow of credit to service the economy has dropped dramatically, driving up costs of short-term loans, threatening to cause what *The Economist* dramatically terms a global financial heart attack. But, the world is not short of liquidity. In fact, the opposite is true. Before the crisis, the market was awash with money. What is crucially in short supply is not so much liquidity as trust in the financial system.

It is comforting to know that central bankers have gathered to coordinate their measures to restore trust and confidence. Though politically unpopular, governments have acted decisively and swiftly to bail out the crucial financial institutions to prevent the financial system from collapsing. Some suggest other additional measures. For example, the US Federal Reserve or Treasury could offer insurance policies of mortgage-backed securities which are already valued at very low prices.[3]

The fourth reason is something interesting. For the first time, the West is conceding to the emerging economies its traditional role in modern economy in deciding the fate of world economy. The emerging economies are asked to play the white knight to rescue the world economy in distress. While the Western economies have slipped into painful recession, many of the emerging economies in East Asia are in reasonably good shape. The Asian countries, thanks to the crucible test of the Asian financial crisis a decade ago, have learned their lessons. China has the potential to play a positive role. It has $2 trillion of foreign reserves, budget surplus for years, and (thank goodness) not integrated to the international financial system. It can easily run budget deficits to pump money to stimulate the economy. The high growth will support the commodity prices of other developing countries. Both India and Brazil have plenty of foreign reserves to tide over this difficult period. Russia has US$550 billion of reserves.

The fifth reason can be found in the modern supply chain management pioneered by electronic business. The relationship between inventory investment and business cycles is a complex one. In the network economy, supply chain management supports a production schedule driven by demand, or made to order. The inventories are minimal, if not zero. In the event of a possible economic downturn, a production firm has no inventory of raw materials and finished products to trim. Even though the demand is lower, the production firms must continue to buy raw materials from their suppliers in order to produce goods for their customers. Their suppliers would not suddenly lose huge chunks of business. They would earn less profit but they would have more time to adjust. Just-in-time production and consumption will lower economic volatility. In the old economy, production firms would drastically cut orders from their supplies, preferring to use up first inventories, thereby exacerbating impacts of a recession.

The last reason can be found in the *longue durée* of history. Economic crises were often the result of wars, epidemics and natural disasters as well as political misrule. Unfortunately, some regions in the world today still suffer from wars and political misrule. The good news is that most parts of the world today enjoy peace. We are far from the circumstances of the late 1920s and 1930s. Europe was then emerging from the devastation of World War I and was driven into World War II by its unresolved problems.

The above are just arguments. No matter how sensible and convincing the arguments, they carry weight only when backed up with real world evidence. To quote Kurt Lewin, "There is nothing more practical than a good theory." Since the Great Depression, the world has seen many financial crises; some of them have led to painful recession. Yet, the rich world has not experienced any depression. Depression occurred in the Third World. For example, depression hit Latin America in the 1980s. The three biggest economies in the region, namely Argentina, Brazil and Mexico, suffered a drop in investment ranging from 17 to 44% during the period 1981–1984.[4] For the region as a whole, open unemployment shot up by 40% between 1980 and 1984. The impact of the crisis was so far-reaching that a decade later in 1992, average real incomes were below the 1981 levels and financial dislocation persisted.[5]

The depression could have been avoided had the governments adopted the Keynesian approach then. Though these policy tools were well known and well tested, one would have thought they were employed. "Quite the contrary: macroeconomic policy, especially in the hands of the International Monetary fund (IMF), was instead employed to impose severe government budget cuts and labor market austerity and eliminate price control. That is, it accelerated the contractionary spiral."[6]

With the demise of Wall Street icons like Lehman Brothers and the near collapse of Citigroup, the intellectual influence of the Anglo-Saxon version of free market economic thinking has also declined. The crisis prompts all of us to examine once again the merits and demerits of various strains of free market thinking. It is a bad time for businessmen but it is an interesting time for the John Keynes of the 21st century to leave their enduring marks.

CHAPTER 4

Financial Engineering or What Can Go Wrong Will

A term that keeps popping up in media reports on the financial crisis is "derivatives". As the term implies, derivatives are financial instruments whose values are *derived* from some underlying entities. These entities can be stocks, commodities, bonds, interest rates, foreign exchange rates, stock market index, consumer price index, or even other derivatives. Derivatives were originally developed to help businesses hedge risks in uncertain business environments, just like we buy car insurance. Nowadays, derivatives are designed with the help of advanced mathematics. A new discipline known as financial engineering has emerged to conduct research and train people to apply mathematical tools for product and process innovation.

One well-known derivative is commodity futures. For example, it can be used by an airline company which wants to hedge uncertainty in oil prices. The airline can sign a futures contract with an oil supplier to buy a specified amount of oil at a specified price over a certain period of time in the future. If the price decreases in the specified period, the airline loses out and the oil supplier gains, or vice versa. But at the point of signing the contract, both sides wish to reduce their future risk so that they are in a better position to make future business plans. There still remains a residual risk in the contract. What if either party goes bankrupt during the period? One convenient solution is to trade the futures in a stock exchange. But, this can only be done if the contract follows the format and standard set by the exchange. Alternatively, a third party can enter the picture to insure a futures contract, a kind of second order insurance. What if this third party collapses, leaving its counterparties with worthless contracts? To reduce the risk, the financial market can establish a clearing-house as part of the financial infrastructure to trade this second order insurance.

In terms of the design goals, derivatives serve as valuable financial instruments to reduce risks of doing business in an uncertain world. Buying insurance to cope with risks is a practice well-known to us. In fact, the traffic laws require that a vehicle can only be on the roads if it is covered by insurance. Insurance is certainly a great innovation used to spread risk and in the case of life insurance to provide financial protection for the dependents of the policy holders. Insurance is a specialized branch of business.

Though derivatives have its origin as financial instruments to limit risk, they have recently become investment products that attract both private and institutional investors. Fortune seems to smile on them until the unexpected happens. Billions are lost overnight; century-old financial firms turn belly-up or are absorbed by their juniors; credit dries up; the global financial markets plunge into an abyss. As a general introduction of what can go wrong, we shall illustrate this point using the case of securitization.

Securitization and How It Can Go Wrong

Securitization is deeply implicated in the current credit crunch. Both securitization and derivative are innovations of financial engineering. Derivative is a product innovation while securitization is a process innovation. It is a beautiful concept to make loans more accessible and cheaper by spreading credit risks from one lender to the community of investors. Traditionally, a bank lends money to creditworthy clients and holds the debts on its book. To reduce risk to the bank, the borrower uses his assets as collateral. The bank uses short-term loans (usually bank deposits) of lower interest to make long-term loans of higher interest. If all goes well, the bank will earn enough from the interest margin to cover its costs and yield a profit. The disadvantage of this traditional approach is that financial firms may not have enough money at their disposal to lend to all borrowers. A promising business may not get loans to expand its activities or a young couple may not be able to buy their dream house. This disadvantage is overcome by securitization which pools the loans together and repackages them to individual or institutional investors. If the loans are mortgages, these repackaged financial products are known as mortgage-backed securities.

The loans no longer stay on the books of the bank which earns a management fee in the process. The risk held originally by the bank is now spread thinly among the community of investors. Risk is reduced while the credit reservoir is broadened and deepened. Though risk is reduced for a particular market player, the aggregate risk of the system is increased. The risk appetite of investors grows when the going is good and, as we soon see, due diligence is often not exercised. The risk is increased further when the financial product is not transparent and is closely linked to other markets.

As Murphy's Law warns us, anything that can go wrong will go wrong. This is especially so when human greed and folly conspire to pervert the ideal serene conceptual beauty of securitization. This is well-illustrated by the subprime debacle. The original loan provider begins to relax his due diligence in checking the creditworthiness of mortgage applicants. In the absence of strict regulation, this is a rational move by mortgage banks. After all, the more relaxed the check on borrower's financial background, the bigger the transaction volume. The bigger the transaction volume, the bigger the profits. This practice gives birth to the term subprime mortgage which means loan made to a house loan applicant with low creditworthiness. In one extreme case, a couple obtained a loan of $1.5 million for a house which they paid $1.16 million. The delighted couple withdrew $333,000 to spend and lived in the nice house for three months. They then moved out, quite happy to give up the newly-bought house.[1]

The subprime crisis is slowly nurtured by loose monetary policy. With low interest rates and accessible mortgages, house prices begin to rise. Builders respond by building more houses as if the party will last forever. Real estate developers enter the mortgage business and aggressively push mortgages to borrowers to boost house sales.[2] Existing house owners feel rich. They use the resident assets as collateral to borrow more to spend. A bubble is slowly building up.

Even though securitization aims at spreading risk, it does not always work that way. As it turned out, many banks that originated mortgage securities somehow did not repackage and sell them to the money market.[3] They were caught with too much risk on the books when the lightning struck.

The 1990s saw new financial innovations in the form of collateralized debt obligations or CDOs. They are the bundling of assets-based securities into different tranches with different credit ratings, interest rate payments, and priority repayment. The subprime-repackaged mortgage can be divided into AAA tranche, mezzanine tranche and subordinated tranche, with the AAA tranche considered the safest with the lowest interest yield. The financial whiz kids use the CDOs as underlying assets and repackage them to produce CDOs-squared. The process can be repeated and we have CDOs-cubed. To complicate matters further, there are also CDOs of credit default swaps. We are entering a financial landscape of high leverage, high risks, and low transparency. As long as the interest rates remain low and the house prices continue to climb, the going is good. Caution is thrown out of the window while the party goes on.

Disaster strikes when subprime defaults and foreclosures increase in numbers. Holders of subordinate tranche CDOs started to unload their worldly goods, triggering a panic reaction of holders of safer CDOs. The party ended abruptly with fire sales of all kinds of CDOs, including those of corporate bonds. Meanwhile, house prices continued their descend, exacerbating the chaos and downward spiral. Issuers of credit default swaps suddenly realized that they could not find the money to pay those who had bought their insurance. Financial firms operate by borrowing on short-term on low interests and lend out long term on higher interests. When their debtors call *en masse* to want their money back when they cannot get rid of their long-term assets in time, we have a classic case of a bank run.

Financial Weapons of Mass Destruction

The market in derivatives has exploded in recent years. The phenomenal growth of derivatives may be led by three factors. First and foremost, it is a highly leveraged and very risky financial instrument. Speculators love it as a means to make a quick profit. Second, the fees are huge. Finally, it operates in a lightly regulated environment. In 2007, some $45 trillion of derivative contracts were traded on the S&P 500 indexes alone. This is four and a half times the total value of the American stock market which is worth approximately $10 trillion.[4]

According to the Bank for International Settlements, the notional value of all outstanding global derivative contracts at the end of 2007 stood at $600 trillion, some 11 times of the world's economic output.[5] A decade earlier, it was only $75 trillion and 2.5 times of global GDP. The fastest growing part of these markets was credit-default swaps. The notional value of credit-default swaps almost doubled in 2007 to $62 trillion.[6]

As a result of the explosive growth, the financial infrastructure cannot keep up with it. The great success of credit default swaps has led to processing backlogs and errors. Some over-the-counter derivatives cannot find a clearing house to trade them and spread out the risks.

Some traditional derivatives like futures are easy to design and understand. However, there are many newer products that are designed by people trained in advanced mathematics and who are often humorously referred to as rocket scientists. Their intellectual outputs are highly specialized and extremely complex products that few understand, often not even their own boss. Nobel laureate Robert Merton, finance professor at Harvard, observes that one of the problems at large financial institutions is the knowledge gap between executives and financial engineers. Though the fate of their firms depends crucially on the derivative business, many executives have never even taken a course in the fundamentals of evaluating complex financial instruments.[7] Things would not have been so bad if the rating agencies had done the work they claim to do. As it turned out, they failed to supply financial markets with intelligence that was authoritative, objectives and credible.

As a result of the lure of huge profits, lack of adequate infrastructure, complexity and poor management supervision, we have a perilous situation. "Large amounts of risk have become concentrated in the hands of relatively few derivatives dealers, which can trigger serious systemic problems," warns Warren Buffett, the legendary investor. This is well-illustrated by the case of American Insurance Group (AIG) which was, without its derivative adventure, a generally safe and well-run insurer. Trouble began when its financial products division, which accounted for just a fraction of its revenues, wrote enough derivatives contracts to destroy the firm and shake the world. With this in mind, we can appreciate why Mr. Buffett describes derivatives as the "financial weapons of mass destruction."

The legendary investor is known for his witty humor and the value of his comments on the financial market, having made his fortune through investment. Here are some of his comments on derivatives.[8]

He sees derivatives as an investment "time bomb". He observes that the rapidly growing trade in derivatives poses a 'mega-catastrophic risk' for the economy. Derivatives generate reported earnings that are often wildly overstated and based on estimates whose inaccuracy may not be exposed for many years. Derivatives also pose a dangerous incentive for false accounting, Mr. Buffett says. The profits and losses from derivates deals are booked straightaway, even though no actual money changes hand. In many cases, the real costs only hit companies many years later. He warns that derivatives can push companies onto a "spiral that can lead to a corporate meltdown", like the demise of the notorious hedge fund Long-Term Capital Management.

Besides the views of the business world, we have the view of management guru Peter Drucker on derivatives. "They are designed to make the trader's speculations more profitable and at the same time less risky — surely a violation of the basic laws of risk and unlikely to work. In fact, they are unlikely to work better than the inveterate gambler's equally 'scientific' systems for beating the odds at Monte Carlo or Las Vegas — as a good many traders have already found out."[9]

Financial Excesses

In some way, derivatives are like medicines. If used appropriately, they are very beneficial. However, used in excess and in ways that depart from the original intention, it can lead to very unpleasant consequences. We have known all kinds of problems that arises from drugs abuse. It does not only bring harm to the person concerned, but to his family, the friends around him and even to society. Using the term "financial excesses" to refer to reckless speculation involving the use of derivatives is in this sense very appropriate.

CHAPTER 5

Financial Architecture — I

Financial crises are generally caused by the interaction between weaknesses in the domestic sector of countries and free flow of international capital, magnified by financial innovations and speeded up by advanced information technology. They can be the result of long periods of macroeconomic policy excesses, persistent capital account deficits, stock market bubbles, housing market bubbles or a combination of a weak financial system and concerted attacks by speculators. In the wake of such crises, there are calls to build a robust and resilient financial system, with sound financial architecture. This chapter and the subsequent one cover some of the key issues in the construction of a sound financial architecture.

A Robust and Sound Financial Sub-System

The financial market is a strange creature, more mysterious than the proverbial elephant to the group of blind men. Free flows of capital make it easier for individuals and firms to access money, which may or may not lead to higher productivity. Financial markets are efficient means for allocation of financial resources. At the same time, the financial system is inherently unstable. Periods of stability tend to lead to financial excesses which often end up in financial crisis and economic recession thereafter. The economist Hyman Minsky argued that economic stability encouraged even greater leverage and excessive debt commitment. The challenge is to design a system with the following features:

- efficient allocation of money for proper consumption and productive investment,
- a payment system that continues to function properly even during financial crises,
- credit that is available to firms so that they can conduct their businesses without disruption,
- risk that is spread evenly and broadly to those who are able to bear it, without increasing the risk for the system.

The proposed financial architecture has a three-tier system. The first tier is a banking and payment subsystem which is made up of banks run in a conservative manner, like the post banks of the past. Deposits are guaranteed and customers earn low interest while credits are given to very low-risk clients. The regulation here is very tight.

The second tier is made up of insurance firms and commercial banks where the regulation ranges from tight to moderate. They are allowed to indulge in low-risk to moderately risky business. They are required to build up their resources during good times in order to meet their obligations during bad times, based on time honored actuarial practices. In times of financial crisis, the state may bail them out by buying their assets if they are likely to survive in ordinary times.

The third tier consists of other financial firms like private banks, merchant banks and investment banks. Though they are the least regulated of the three categories of financial firms, they are still subjected to the criteria of transparency and spreading of risks. In times of financial crisis, they cannot expect help in any form from the state.

Payment System Consisting of Narrow Banks

The core of the payment system is made up of banks which operate pretty much like post banks of the good old days. In other words, they are the banks with a narrow focus. All the deposits are fully guaranteed by the state. The depositors earn a relatively low interest. These core banks lend out money to low-risk borrowers. Core banks are local banks, with no overseas branches. They have branches all over the country, housed in modest premises. To cut cost, they rely a lot on Internet and telephone banking to run their operations.

Their customers are likely to be government agencies, schools, non-profit organizations, and risk-averse individuals. Business firms would also have accounts with the banks for the purpose of using them as payment systems.

The key concepts are efficiency, robustness, and fail-safeness. The analogy is like running a telephone system that has to be on the air all the time. Shareholders of these banks are forewarned that they cannot expect their investment to earn huge profits. In the same vein, board of directors and senior managers are selected based on their commitment to public service, integrity and prudence.

Core banks serve as safe havens for depositors in times of financial turmoil. Bank withdrawals from weak banks are re-deposited in the core banks. The level of aggregate bank reserves is thus maintained. In such situations, bank runs on weak banks will not produce instability in the banking system.[1] This ensures that the credit and payment systems can continue to function uninterrupted.

Though the system of core banks would operate as the robust payment system, they are unable to meet the needs of business firms and those with more complex financial needs. For these needs, we need insurance companies and commercial banks.

Insurance Companies and Commercial Banks

Insurance companies have built up a body of knowledge that has withstood the test of time. The business model adopts a long-term view. They have lots of historical data as well as actuarial science to help them decide on the premium to charge for a certain policy. As long as they exercise prudence, eschew undue risk-taking and use financial engineering instruments appropriately, they are unlikely to get into trouble.

Insurance companies have an important role in the general social and economic life. For example, airlines cannot fly their plane unless the plane is insured. You cannot drive your car on the road unless it has insurance coverage. Insurance firms are privileged in the sense that such legal requirements create a big and stable market for their products and services. They also act as pension funds when they sell life insurance to customers. If they sell health insurance, they effectively act as part of the national health services. For all these reasons, insurance firms are to operate under strict supervision.

Like insurance companies, commercial banks also have a long history of experience to guide their business operations. They take deposits from their customers and loan out the money to credit-worthy clients. The state guarantees up to a certain amount of the deposits. In return for this privilege, commercial banks are regulated, though not as tightly as the core banks. As long as they exercise prudence and due diligence, they can make an honest living by lending to healthy businesses as well as credit-worthy households and individuals.

Commercial banks can learn much from the Spanish banks in their banking regulations and relatively conservative banking practices. During the boom period, the central bank requires other banks to increase their provision in case of loan defaults — a countercyclical measure. When banks set up off-balance-sheet Special Investment Vehicle, the central bank requires them to take a capital charge large enough to render attempts to go around banking regulations unattractive.

If a commercial bank takes excessive risk and is going bust in bad times, it cannot expect a bailout from the state. All that the state can do is to refund up to a certain amount the money of the depositors, advise them to transfer the money to the core banks and let the errant bank disappear. This is to reduce the ever recurrent problems associated with moral hazard.

Other Financial Firms

Under this rubric will fall merchant banks, private banks, investment banks and venture capital firms. They are not allowed to take deposits. Though they are lightly regulated, it does not mean that they can do what they like. They still have to abide by the general regulations of running a business.

These financial firms are the most innovative, and have a penchant for risk-taking. They are the whiz kids of financial engineering. They are the avid seekers of opportunities and if they get it right, they are well-rewarded. And if they get it wrong? Bank regulation and supervision are intended not to stop them from making mistakes, but to make sure that if they get into a nasty mess, they do not hurt the innocent parties and cause a meltdown of the financial system. To this end, they are allowed to take risks to the extent that they can bear the full cost of it themselves. (This is similar to allowing a risk-loving driver to take part in the Formula One race but not allowing him to have fellow passengers). They are not allowed to make inflated claims. They are also required to explicitly reveal the perils when they are courting their clients to buy the related financial products.

They run their business like any other businesses. The fate of the business is mainly in the hands of their shareholders and the managers appointed by them. Buyers of their bonds are also forewarned that they do face the danger of loan default just like they buy any other commercial papers.

These firms will not expect bailout or any other forms of state assistance in times of difficulties. However, the state can help to set up clearing houses so that no specific firm is caught with too many obligations.

Does this mean that these firms are unable to earn an honest living? Far from it, as Peter Drucker pointed out in an article, *Innovate or Die*,[2] there are areas where these firms can render value-adding services and make a fair profit.

Key Features of the Proposed Financial Architecture

The proposed setup ensures that the payment system continues to operate in times of financial crises. It serves as the most basic infrastructure of the financial system. The business seems boring but it is crucial. It is unlikely to attract people who enjoy tackling new problems at the job. There is little room for innovation except in the area of efficiency enhancement and improvement of what the staff knows well.

However, the setup has room for some initiative and innovation. They are found in insurance firms and commercial banks. These firms operate on time-honored principles and practices. As long as they are prudent and exercise due diligence, they are going to earn an honest living while rendering a vital service to the economic well-being of society.

For the risk takers and advantage seekers, there is the sector of merchant banks and investment banks, private banks and venture capital firms. Here, one is able to exercise one's talent in coming up with new products and services. It does not mean, however, that it is free for all, without any supervision at all. The supervision is lax, restricted to the prevention of systemic meltdown of the financial system and to the protection of the innocent.

Financial Infrastructure

The ongoing financial crisis has shaken the global financial system to the core, leading to deep and painful recession in most countries. It reveals a simple and ugly truth, namely the current financial system based on the free market principles of the Anglo-American brand has serious flaws. Rich individuals have discovered the danger of leaving their monies with Wall Street firms. Amidst the woes, there is an opportunity for Asia. Asian financial centers like Hong Kong, Singapore, and Tokyo can strive to build a reputation as centers where Ponzi schemes will be nabbed at the bud and where financial products of good quality thrive. If they can be bold enough to redesign their financial architecture so that they are sound and stable, and robust especially in times of financial crises, they may become preferred centers of the global financial market.

This is all the more likely given that Asia is the center of economic action in the 21st century. This Asian financial system is not going to replace the current international financial system, but it will function as a sub-system, by working closely with it. In times of great stress and turbulence, it can act as an oasis of stability and tranquility, serving the needs of business firms all over the world.

CHAPTER 6

Financial Architecture — II

The previous chapter describes a financial infrastructure that aims to support a robust and stable financial system. That, in itself is not enough. It needs a set of policies that looks at risk management and interaction between the different components. Issues at this level are conveyed in press reports by keywords such as risk, contagion, innovation, excesses and speculation.

Risk is a key factor of financial system stability and it can be managed in many ways. One recent innovation is to spread the risk burden more thinly to more parties. Yet, this has not produced the robustness people hoped for. The situation is made worse when rating agencies fail to provide a fair assessment of the risk profile of different financial products. Another source of system fragility comes in the form of contagion. There is also the question of unregulated banking in the form of offshore banking.

Higher Level of Systemic Risk

In an earlier chapter, we have seen how securitization has led to a lower standard of prudence in writing loans. Some may take comfort in the fact that this financial engineering method also disperses risk to a wider group of investors. The dispersion of risks should ideally reduce the severity of financial crisis. Unfortunately, the end results are the opposite, for two reasons. First, if people are not prone to take more risk, the dispersion of risks may have the desired result of a more stable financial system. As it turns out, risk-spreading financial instruments have encouraged investors to take on greater and greater risks. The end result is that we have a financial system "bursting with risks at its seams." The unintended consequence of spreading risk has increased risk for the system as a whole.[1]

Second, the perceived reduction of risks decreases asset price volatility. This in turn encourages players to take on more leverage to buy assets, thereby driving up prices.[2] This leads to asset inflation thus increasing the size of the bubble.

Another contributing factor is the use of impersonal statistical methods of credit assessment. By replacing credit assessment based on personal, cumulative knowledge of the credit history and characters of borrowers, the new approach has dramatically increased risks.[3]

Undue risk exposure can bring down a firm. It can inflict carnage to its business partners. Risk management at firm, national or international levels needs to identify players, financial instruments, products and activities that tend to increase risks. What appears wonderful in theory may turn out to carry with it a bag of toxic spray.

Independent Rating Agencies

Investors rely on rating agencies as an important source of information before making decisions. This makes sense as individual and even corporate investors are not in a position to gain access to all relevant and important data for evaluating the quality of a product. But, what happens if the rating agencies fail to do what they claim? Here lies a weak link in the decision making process.

Currently, a rating agency earns its fees from firms who pay the agency to produce a report about their own financial health or the quality of their product. There is an obvious conflict of interests. How can the agency be expected to produce an independent and objective report about a firm when it is paid by the firm to produce the report? The rating agency is unlikely to do so. The result is that many investors who place their trust in the reports have lost their shirts.

A better alternative is to set up independent and specialized rating agencies funded by the whole financial industry as a part of the financial infrastructure. When a firm wants to issue bonds, it needs to pay the fee to the financial authorities who will decide which rating agency to hire to do the independent study.

Contagion and Currency Control

The international financial system is a system with different components interacting with each other. The result is that the whole is more than the sum of the parts. However, the gains come with a price. A problem originating in one aspect of the system is transmitted to other aspects. The more closely integrated the system is, the faster and deeper the transmission. The system can be so seriously affected that it may collapse. We have seen this happening in computer systems. A computer virus can crash the mail system of millions of users all over the world in a few hours. System designers therefore use checks and controls at the boundaries of the components and sub-systems to reduce the risk of such contagion. We have seen this at work in airports as a matter of routine. Similar techniques were in use during the SARS epidemic. Importers of pets into a country must be prepared to let their pets being quarantined and observed for a while. Such measures are precautionary in nature. Although they introduce some degree of inefficiency and waste, these are accepted for the greater good.

The idea of checks and control is also applicable to the international financial system. To reduce the risk of contagion, some degree of separation among the sub-systems is necessary. This is particularly useful for small economies with huge exposure to the international economy. Even if their fundamentals are right, they are always exposed to the danger of currency crisis in times of turbulence. For example, if foreign investors assess that a financial crisis is coming, they will sell their equities and convert their assets into an international currency. This explains the rise of US dollar during the current crisis. By selling the local currency to buy dollars or Euros, the local currency loses ground. This is a pattern that has been repeated many times, and currency speculators know it. If a group of them gang up to attack a certain currency by selling short, that small country is going to face a currency crisis, even though the fundamentals are strong. A useful method is to shield the local currency from such speculation by currency control. It is not a perfect shield as there are loopholes to exploit. The control is not watertight and there will be some leakage, but it is able to stop the uncontrolled flow and arrest currency crisis. Indeed, capital account liberalization must not be embraced before banks have proper risk management system, effective supervision of financial institutions and prudent macroeconomic policies.[4]

Capital flow control of a country is a way to contain the risk of contagion by reducing the scope and depth of its integration with the global financial system. It certainly makes money flow more inefficiently but it does not really affect FDI and other long-term investments as well as trade. Cases in point are the experiences of China and Malaysia. During the Asian financial crisis, the then Malaysian Prime Minister, Dr. Mahathir, imposed currency controls against the advice of the IMF. Though the move evoked a chorus of hue and cry from the Western media initially, it has since been seen as an important factor for the quick recovery of the Malaysian economy.

To borrow a term often used by software engineers, we live in a cruel and dirty world. To build a robust and stable system, they must make compromises and trade-offs, for example, by sacrificing efficiency for reliability. In the case of the international financial system, foreign exchange markets are a source of financial instability. Volatility in these markets is a result of speculative activities.[5]

Let us look at some figures. According to the Bank for International Settlement, the *average daily* turnover in global foreign exchange markets was $3.2 trillion in 2007. The volume of world trade is at $12 trillion *per year.*

There is a flood of money flowing around the globe every day — many times more than the amount needed for trade and investment. Some of the money is used for hedging against currency fluctuations, thereby playing a useful role. The bulk of the foreign exchange transactions are accounted for by speculation, estimated at 70% to 90%.[6]

To discourage currency speculations from causing havoc, Chile has imposed a tax on short-term capital inflows.[7] Small countries and those with weak financial systems can learn from its experience.

Offshore Banking

One weak spot in the global financial system is offshore banking, which is operating in a non-regulated environment. Though most offshore banks are domiciled in island states, the biggest among them are housed in Switzerland and Luxembourg. To the general public, offshore banking is associated with money laundering, drug money, secret bank accounts, safe havens for organized crime and tax evasion. After September 11, it has been accused of helping international terrorist groups move their money around. Such features would qualify offshore banking to be an important part of the international financial system. The additional data below would tell us that it not only plays an important role, it is crucially important to the system.

It is estimated that as much as half of the world's capital flows through offshore banking centers. They are custodians of 26% of the world's wealth, including 31% of the net profits of American multinational companies.[8] With such volume handled by financial institutions operating in a non-regulated environment, one can imagine the kind of havoc it can create when the players bet wrongly. This is precisely what has happened. As pointed out by Nobel economics laureate Paul Krugman, the crisis for the most part, has not involved problems with deregulated institutions that took new risks. "Instead, it has involved risks taken by institutions that were never regulated in the first place."[9]

Given its potential to be a source of trouble, one cannot understand why such a large part of global banking can be left uncontrolled. The plausible answer lies in the fact that the arrangement caters to the interests of the super-rich and powerful. The Nobel economics laureate and former chief economist of the World Bank, Joseph Stiglitz, recalls how the US authorities rejected the proposal of OECD to improve the transparency of offshore banking centers. This is certainly not in tandem with the US's enthusiasm to preach and impose good corporate governance on the rest of the world.[10]

Neither is it too difficult to squeeze offshore banking and reduce its role to the minimum. Joseph Stiglitz points out, "You ask why, if there's an important role for a regulated banking system, do you allow a non-regulated banking system to continue? It's in the interest of some of the moneyed interests to allow this to occur. It's not an accident; it could have been shut down at any time. If you said the US, the UK, the major G7 banks will not deal with offshore bank centers that don't comply with G7 banks regulations, these banks could not exist. They only exist because they engage in transactions with standard banks."[11]

Trust and Confidence

One cardinal principle in banking and finance is that the people must have trust in the banks and confidence in the financial system. Even though the world is still awash with liquidity, financial firms are finding it very difficult to find credit simply because trust and confidence have evaporated. The current crisis has shown once again that the global financial system is fragile and unstable.

The onus is on the capital market which has to work hard to restore public trust and confidence. One important move in this direction is to reform and construct a more resilient and sound financial system.

CHAPTER 7

Reforming IMF — from Fire Fighting to Fire Prevention

The International Monetary Fund (IMF) was established as part of the Bretton Woods institutions designed at the end of the World War II to deal with global economic matters. The other two were the World Bank and General Agreement on Tariff and Trade (GATT). Between them, they aim to foster global monetary cooperation, secure financial stability, facilitate international trade, promote high employment and sustainable economic growth, and reduce poverty. More specifically, the explicit *raison d'être* of the IMF is to provide financial assistance to countries that suffer serious balance-of-payment difficulties. It is interesting to note that the Fund behaves like an onlooker in the current crisis (at least until mid-October 2008), unlike that overworked participant in the Asian financial crisis.

More than six decades have passed since the birth of the IMF and the economic and financial landscape of the world has since changed radically, almost beyond recognition. The size of the global financial market has exploded while the money at the Fund's disposal has only grown incrementally. There have been repeated calls from various stakeholders to reform the IMF, the latest being made at the G20 meeting in November 2008. The leaders of the emerging economies wish to have more say in formulating the world's financial rules. One obvious issue is increasing the voting rights of developing countries. Such demand is finding some sympathetic ears among the rich countries. For example, French President Nicolas Sarkozy wanted emerging economies like China and India to exercise more clout in global economic decision making.[1] However, there is something more fundamental than power-sharing, and this has to do with how the world should look at itself.

Our point of departure may be stated as follows. First, all countries in the world have a shared destiny. It is in the enlightened self-interest of the rich countries to help the poor countries, especially when the latter are in financial crisis and dire economic conditions. Second, in times of financial crises, the IMF must first consider the well-being of the poorest strata in these countries. Third, the stated goals of the IMF must be carried out within such an overarching framework.

Set against our position, the track record of the IMF has left much to be desired. During the Cold War period, the IMF supported military regimes that were friendly to Western business interests. When Third World countries faced financial crises and turned to the IMF, help came with stringent conditions. Instead of an expansionary approach employed by the rich countries in crisis, the poor countries were required to follow tight fiscal and monetary policies. Such austerity programs hurt the poor the hardest. This goes against humanitarian values that are so often championed by the West in international rhetoric. The policies even drove economic recession into depression, as evident in Latin American countries in the 1980s. On this point alone, the IMF would find it hard to fend off the charge that it has been practicing double standards.

One may wonder why the IMF acted in the way it did? Poor countries get into balance-of-payment difficulties for a variety of reasons. Quite often, they are unable to service their loans borrowed from international banks. These countries are then offered financial assistance by the Fund with conditions attached. They must restructure their economies by curbing import and increasing export, cutting subsidies and slashing public expenditure. In the short-term, this may increase their foreign reserves to service the loans. No wonder critics maintain that the IMF behaves more like the fairy Godmother of creditor international banks than a friend of needy nations. Critics may be more right than wrong. The biggest rescue packages of the IMF went to countries where the exposure of American banks was the greatest, as shown by two researchers of University of North Carolina.[2] During the Asian financial crisis a decade ago, the US administration used the IMF to push for the US economic policy.[3]

It must be noted that the contributions of rich countries to the IMF come from taxpayers, not from big banks. When these banks fail to exercise prudence and lend money to country X, it is their problem when X fails to pay back the loan. The IMF can only function as the lender of last resort for country X, and not as the protector of these international banks. Doing otherwise can only promote moral hazard, a disease so common among irresponsible bankers.

Viewed from long-term perspective, the IMF does not seem to be very clever. By driving poor countries into destitution, the Fund is also acting against the enlightened self-interests of the rich countries. It destroys market for their products, cultivates animosity against them. Worse still, the IMF creates conditions for the emergence of failed states. It has certainly not enhanced the image of the Fund. Its reputation was further dented in the Asian financial crisis when its prescriptions proved to be wrong.

Partly because of their bad experiences with the Fund, emerging economies have piled up huge foreign reserves. Their policy carries an opportunity cost of nearly 1% of GDP, according to Professor Dani Rodrik of Harvard University.[4] At the same time, it allows Uncle Sam to live beyond his means, which is certainly not in his long-term interest. In short, it is bad for everybody.

The current financial crisis may prove to be an important chapter in the biography of the IMF. The G20 summit is at once important symbolically and in substance. The emerging economies have joined the high table of economic powers and with it the burden of responsibilities. Would they, particularly China, be able to champion the welfare of the poor countries and the enlightened interest of the rich countries? A week before the G20 summit in November 2008, the British Prime Minister, Gordon Brown, called on China and the oil-rich Gulf states to pump more resources into an IMF bailout fund. While China does not rule out any possible funding commitment, China finds it more beneficial to stimulate its own domestic economy.[5] By maintaining high growth, China will be able to provide a market for its trading partners, in particular the commodities producers. At the same time, leaders of some emerging economies see the crisis as an occasion to call for a reform of the international financial system.[6]

There are two ways richer emerging economies can do to help other Third World countries cope with their balance-of-payment problems. They can *directly* render financial aid to the latter, thereby bypassing the IMF and reducing its influence. Or, they can do so via the IMF on the condition that the Fund let them have their fair share of voting rights.

We are in favor of the second option. Instead of letting the IMF wither into irrelevance, it is better to remodel it to play new roles. Change is both necessary and inevitable. The IMF can certainly learn from its sister organization, the World Bank, which has morphed into a knowledge bank and a promoter of global public good. Besides being a fire fighter, the IMF should reinvent itself as an authority in fire prevention. Fire prevention requires another set of skills and responsibility. Conflagration prevention in the financial market means building an international financial system that is sound, stable and robust. It entails close collaboration with the central banks of various countries, the Bank for International Settlements, global banks and financial firms to redesign the international financial system. The new architecture must promote *productive* investment and trade, protect the interests of poor countries, tame currency speculation, discourage financial excesses and encourage counter-cyclical financial practices. This is not an easy job. As noted earlier in this chapter, the firefighter was glaringly absent when the fires were raging furiously in the US and Europe. The reason is clear. The Fund carries little clout with these rich countries and the water in its reservoir is far from adequate to dampen the fire. How the Fund can succeed will depend on how the emerging economies and the rich countries wish to see the world.

CHAPTER 8

Regulation and Deregulation

A financial system is a socio-economic system embedded in a bigger matrix of legal, economic and political institutions. It is part of the whole complex of the free market economy with different interests where the manufacturing interests converge as well as diverge with financial interests. This is why the US administration refers to the need to reconcile the interests of Main Street and Wall Street. Even within the financial industry, there are convergence and divergence of interests among various players. As the focus of the current financial crisis is on banks and financial firms, we would discuss their regulation and deregulation.

During the Gold Standard period from 1880 to 1913, banking crises were fairly limited. This period also had fairly open global financial system. After the Depression of the 1930s, the governments of the rich countries began to regulate their banks and financial firms. The regulation stayed pretty much in place until the 1960s. It was a period of boring calm. Until the collapse of the Bretton Woods system in 1971, there was no banking crisis except one in Brazil in 1962.[1]

As a result of the tussle among the various interest groups, there is an observed trend towards deregulation of the financial sector in the past several decades. The 1960s is a transition period from regulation to deregulation in

financial systems. It is part of the persistent and fundamental change of the free market economies. It experienced historically high interest rates for some years.
What is even more notable is that the world has suffered
increasingly frequent and severe bouts of financial instability in the form of financial crisis, stock market booms
and busts, recessions and even depression in the case of
some developing countries.[2]

By the early 1990s, the regulatory system has largely
disappeared. It is either abandoned through the formal
repeal of laws or by means of getting around it with
clever innovations. Financial crises become a regular feature of economic life.[3] There is the credit crunch of 1966,
the Wall Street crash in 1987, the collapse of the Savings
and Loans in 1990. The crises from Mexico (1994), East
Asia (1997), Russia (1998) to Brazil (1999) are shocking
in their frequency, virulence, contagion and scale. The
crises highlight how interconnected and vulnerable the
world's financial systems have become.[4] The most serious
of this series of events is the current global financial crisis
and economic recession, and therefore the most serious
crisis since the Great Depression. It constitutes a defining
moment in the history of international financial system
and economy of our lifetime.

The aftermath of the Asian financial crisis saw the
most serious reconsideration of the structure of the international financial system since the breakdown of the
Bretton Woods system in 1971.[5] It forms part of the continuing talks about reshaping the global financial system
into a robust, stable and resilient system.[6] As it turned
out, the enthusiasm for strengthening the system faded
into the background when the turmoil blew over. But
with the biggest crisis of our lifetime looming larger, the

fervor for reform has returned. High on the list is to do a better job in regulating the industry.

The leaders representing the G20 countries declared in no uncertain terms during their summit in November 2008 the need for financial regulation. Even the pro-market *The Economist* commented that:[7]

> "Regulation is necessary, and much must now be done to improve the laws of finance. But it must be the right regulation: an end to America's fragmented system of oversight; more transparency; capital requirements that lean against booms and flex with busts; supervision of giants, like AIG, that are too big and too inter-connected to fail; accounting that values risks better and that everyone accepts; clearing houses and exchanges to make derivatives safer and less opaque."

Having seen time and again the failures of the rich countries to get their acts together, it is only reasonable to be skeptical about their sincerity, ability and resolve. Perhaps it is irrelevant to ask whether they are sincere or not. In order to save the capitalist system, they may have no choice.

The Pros and Cons of Regulation

The reasons advanced for and against regulation are basically ideological and practical.

Opponents of regulation believe in the self-regulatory mechanism and dynamism of market forces. Markets are not perfect, but they have the magic power to cure them-selves of wrongdoings and excesses. It is almost like Mother Nature, which picks out the fittest to survive in the midst of fierce competition. The end result is that only the best and fittest can thrive in the economic landscape. Based on this position, governments and international bodies like the IMF are the source of the recurring problem of financial crises. A government does its economy a great disservice through its inconsistent macroeconomic policies and bank guarantees which breed moral hazard. The IMF does similar harm by acting as the lender of last resort to bankrupt countries, thereby not encouraging global banks to follow good practices in their lending activities.

At the practical level, criticism is directed at how tight regulation obstructs the banking industry from performing its job properly. Financial resources are not efficiently allocated to productive investment. Businesses have a very limited range of financial instruments to help them cope with vicissitudes in the business environment. Advocates of a lightly-regulated money market argue that free market creates wealth, makes loans easier and cheaper, provides market with liquidity, increases economic efficiency and stabilizes markets.

The prescribed solution is straightforward: let market forces operate and financial crises would be much reduced in severity and frequency.

While the financial industry provides services to society and earns profit in the process, the financial industry has been known to create havoc in the economy and society through its excesses and speculation. Worse still, financial crises hurt hundreds of millions of innocent bystanders who play no part in the financial excesses but suffer when the bubbles burst. Advocates of regulation insist that the financial industry shares similarities with the food, healthcare and transport industries in that they affect the welfare of the people very profoundly.

In democratic societies, such industries can only do so with the consent of society. This is the moral justification for regulation. An unregulated market operates like the jungle, favoring the high and mighty at the expense of the small and weak.

Even though the market may exhibit self-regulatory behavior at the best of times, there are many cases of market failures. Adam Smith, the intellectual father of the free market, knows just too well of the positive roles of market forces. Yet, he explicitly advocates the regulation of banks. He is well aware that bank failures have damaging effects on the economy more generally.[8]

The economist Hyman Minsky observes that capitalist economies have, as normal states of affairs, the following attributes: inherently unstable nature, disequilibrium and unemployment. He says, "The capitalist market mechanism is flawed in the sense that it does not lead to stable price–full employment equilibrium, and the basis of the flaw resides in the financial system."[9] The ups and downs of the economic cycle and fragility of the financial system are aggravated by deregulation, globalization and integration with the help of advanced information technology.

The proposed solution is succinctly stated by Martin Feldstein, former president and CEO of the National Bureau of Economic Research and a former chairman of the President's Council of Economic Advisors.

"The banking system as a whole is a 'public good' that benefits the nation over and above the profits that it earns for the banks' shareholders. Systemic risks to the banking system are risks for the nation as a whole. Although the managements and shareholders of financial institutions are, of course, eager to protect the solvency of their own institutions, they do not adequately take into account the adverse effects to the nation of systemic failure. Banks left to themselves will accept more risk than is optimal from a systemic point of view. That is the basic case for government regulation of banking activity and the establishment of capital requirements."[10]

Limits of Regulation

A sound and robust international financial system, acting as a bedrock to support global economy, is a crucial element of the socio-economic infrastructure. Its central task is to promote trade, investment and economic growth, rather than serving as a platform for speculators to display their talents and use it as a casino. Regulation done in the right way is part of the effort to build a sound and robust financial system.

Though tighter regulation is certainly needed, there is a limit to what regulation can do. As mentioned earlier, the regulation must be correct in the first place.

Secondly, the regulators must not fall prey to corruption, a common political disease in many Asian counties.

Third, banks and financial firms are past masters in exploiting the blind spots and profiting from the loopholes. For example, they can hide their assets off their balance sheets, or buy insurance (credit default swaps) which enable them to evade the capital requirements designed by the regulators.

Fourth, a crisis of such enormity occurs as a result of many causes. Outdated regulation is only one of them. The others are dodgy lending, too much cheap money, government distortion and unreliable reports by rating agencies. Even well designed rules are of not much use when the supervision is not properly conducted, as we see in the Madoff case. The Securities and Exchange Commission failed to oversee the operations of the investment firm. More bizarre still, it was sleeping on complaints received as early as the late 1990s.

Finally, financial regulation is part of the whole matrix of economic structure. If the microeconomic and macro-economic polices are not right in the first place, there is not much financial regulators can do. When the public debt continues to grow out of proportion of the national gross product, there is no running away from the day of reckoning.

CHAPTER 9

Back to Basics

A basic principle in any business is that it must provide value-adding products and services to its customers, within the parameters of social norms and institutions. Ideally, it should also contribute to the benefit of society. This principle obviously applies to banking and finance too.

Profit will be a natural outcome of value-adding the business activity. What is even more important is that the flow of profit will last for a long time under normal circumstances. Of course, it is possible to have huge profits in the short-term by deviating from such value-adding practice, but such an approach will not last. It may even end up getting the business into deep trouble. In fact, we are witnessing this story of the financial industry unfolding before our eyes.

The idea of value-adding is crucial in our understanding of how things can go wrong in financial speculation. Before we elaborate further, it is useful to differentiate between risk taking and speculation. We all know that many activities in life have an element of risk, like cycling or medical operation. But we do not describe them as speculation. Insurance is a well-known financial instrument. By selling a policy, the insurance company takes on certain risks while the buyer reduces the risks by paying a fee. As long as the company exercises prudence and spreads out the risks, it can make money even though it is in a risky business. A financial transaction, conducted within its appropriate goal, adds value to the business. For example, a company hedges its exposure to foreign currencies. The hedge introduces an element of certainty in a turbulent environment and allows the company to plan better. But if the company uses the hedge instrument as a main source of making money, then it is indulging in speculation and is courting trouble. Companies are courting trouble when their treasuries use derivatives as a source of profit. "For a long time now a number of companies have seen their treasury areas as profit centres."[1] There are several giant companies which went bust because of this.

Perhaps the best advice offered to financial firms against using speculation as a way of earning its profit is given by Peter Drucker in his short article *Innovate or Die*.[2] When financial firms' incomes rely more and more on financial speculation, they are slipping into trouble.

> "Every financial-services firm has to do some trading for its own account. It is a routine part of managing the firm's own finances and is aimed at minimizing risk…. But when trading for a firm's own account becomes a big activity, it ceases to be 'trading' and has become 'gambling'. And no matter how clever the gambler, the laws of probability guarantee that he will eventually lose all he gained, and then a good deal more…

No industry can survive, let alone prosper, unless it is paid for services rendered to others, that is, to outside clients and customers. But the customers of the financial firms that trade for their own account are other financial firms trading for their own account. And this is a 'zero-sum game' with one firm's gains being another firm's losses — and nothing left over to pay either's expenses."

Anyone interested in the future of banking and finance would do well to read Peter Drucker's article. Besides giving a sharp warning against excessive trading, he asks banks to take up the challenge to innovate and to earn an honest living by rendering services to others. He has offered a few suggestions in the article. Innovation involves experimentation and it may fail to take off in the harsh reality of the business world. Firms have learned to combine trying out the new with the well-tested, or a combination of exploration and exploitation.[3] In fact, banks can still survive as profitable business by sticking to traditional banking activities such as mergers and acquisitions, divestitures, financing import and export, leasing and currency exchange. With the growth of knowledge and accumulation of experience, such business has become "commodities". In this area, firms will have to compete on the basis of cost management, deep understanding of the clients' needs, cultivation of business relationship and due diligence. Below is a case of how these principles used in a modest outfit can deliver value to the customers and make a decent profit.

Being Boring Still Pays

There is a short report in *The Economist* (April 17th 2004) which should be included in the basic texts of banking and finance. It is about a humble bank in Gammesfeld, a small village in Germany. The Raiffeisenbank Gammesfeld is one of German 1,400-odd co-operative banks. It has a mere € 15m in assets. There are no automatic teller machines and no computers. Mr Vogt, the sole employee of the bank, knows all his customers, and therefore has a fair idea of credit risk. "The Raiffeisenbank Gammesfeld pays a generous 3% interest on savings, regardless of the size of deposit, and charges a mere 4% for mortgages and 5% for other loans. It is no wonder the balance sheet grew by 11% last year. Outsiders often ask to open accounts, but are turned away: "Gammesfelders only."[4] As a financial intermediary, it offers very attractive interest rates for its depositors and borrowers.

The example shows that by sticking to conservative practices, prudence and due diligence, banks can earn an honest living by functioning as a custodian of depositors' money and a provider of credit to financially healthy customers. In Chapter Two, we go through briefly the evolution of banks and financial firms. Even though they have changed dramatically to take on new roles in the course of history, their role as financial intermediaries has not disappeared. As financial intermediaries, banks must enjoy the trust of their clients and customers. To instil such trust, banks have spared no expense to house themselves in solid and magnificent buildings. But from debacles of banks housed in grand buildings, the public have learned that the facade of an imposing building is one thing, the way the business is run is another. As people learn more about how banks should operate, they will be less charmed by architectural splendour of bank buildings. But what should banks do to regain the trust of the public? Surely, public confidence is not inspired by astronomical salaries and bonuses being rewarded to the senior managers when the banks have lost billions during their watch.

The Question of Remuneration

One issue that has caught public attention is the mind-boggling financial rewards enjoyed by senior managers of banks. They are so rewarded because they are "so very good". But why couldn't these financial geniuses prevent their concern from morphing into a financial titanic? Worse still, the top managers could be looking the other way when their firms were throwing caution to the winds and when their traders gamble with other people's money. It does appear to the public that the remuneration scheme is dysfunctional. It is therefore not surprising that financial institutions have been called upon to avoid compensation schemes which reward excessive short-term returns or risk-taking.[5]

But, is it wrong to reward bank employees for the profit they generate through speculation? Let us go through a rather simple example to show how this can land a bank in hot soup in the long run. Two traders TA and TB take two opposite positions. We ignore transaction cost here, for simplicity. After a given period, TA makes $ 200 million while TB loses a similar amount. TB is fired while TA is rewarded $20 million. Repeat this process long enough, and many TBs are fired and many TAs become fat cats. But in the end, the bank is bankrupt. Of course, the actual scenario is much more complicated. Traders take highly leveraged position where a few wrong moves can sink their banks. It is salutary to heed the words of Peter Drucker that the financial banks are trading against each other.[6] It is a zero sum game. In the end, the real winners are the fat cats, while everybody else ends up as losers.

The current crisis provides some materials for reflections. The British Guardian newspaper reports the following data for taxpayers and shareholders to digest.[7] From 2000 to 2007, former Lehman Brothers' boss Dick Fuld was paid $485 million. Merrill Lynch's chairman Stan O'Neal retired after announcing losses of $8 billion but taking a final pay deal worth $161 million in 2007. His CEO colleague John Thain was rewarded with $83 million the same year.[8] Citigroup's boss Chuck Prince left in 2007 with a $38 million pay deal after the bank incurred multibillion dollar losses. Bob Diamond, president of the British bank Barclay, received a salary of £250,000, but his total pay reached £36 million in 2007. Just in case the public need further hints of why some people should be so upset, read some other details in same Guardian report. At one point in October 2008, Morgan Stanley's $10.7 billion pay package for the year was greater than the entire stock market value of the business. At that price, the staff could just use their pay to buy the bank!

In light of what has happened under the watch of those lavishly paid top bank executives, it is easy to understand why many would get inflamed. The same Guardian article contains the following passage,[9]

"Many critics of investment banks have questioned why firms continue to siphon off billions of dollars of bank earnings into bonus pools rather than using the funds to shore up the capital position of the crisis-stricken institutions."

Such anger should not divert us from yet another problem. The huge salaries by the finance industry to the mathematically gifted to devise complicated derivatives has incurred an opportunity cost for society. Let us read the following observation made in a letter to *The Economist.*

"Banks have taken much of the cream of the scientific talent in America and Europe, and to what end? The rush to increase profits has come to naught and in many cases to financial disaster. Imagine what the young people could have done if they had chosen careers in science and medicine. What innovations might have resulted? What breakthroughs might have been achieved? Instead they were used to create a false financial system that is ruinous for our countries."[10]

Two Discussion Points

The financial industry is an archetypical service industry. Though capital is certainly important, what is even more valuable is the trust and confidence it enjoys among its stakeholders — the shareholders, employees, clients and business partners. Like other businesses, the quality of its staff is crucial and it is they who are responsible in building up the brand name of a firm. Besides the issue of pay discussed above, two other points would be discussed here. The first point is whether there is an oversupply of people. The second concerns the background suitable for work in the investment area.

In his article, Peter Drucker observes that "the industry's traditional products and services have been around so long that there is an oversupply of people and firms proficient in them." Judging by the vast expansion of university places in the last decade, the oversupply is likely to worsen. There will always be vacancies as a result of business expansion and replacement for retiring staff. The positions available are taken up by the best and brightest or those who have the right connections. Though we do not have concrete figures, we would invite our readers to look around them and ask their friends. Nowadays, a fresh graduate in banking and finance would be lucky to be trained for a senior management post in future. A fresh graduate is more likely to be assigned to the marketing department to promote sales of financial products to the public. This is not the kind of career that an average Economics or Banking student expects to have. Is there something that banks can do for them? We think so. Banks are in the business of being financial intermediaries. The staff must not only know the fine details of banking products and services, but also the details of the clients — details of the clients' business, their needs, their creditworthiness, which can change with time and circumstances. An intimate knowledge of the clients and their business must form part of a bank's resources, and this takes time and effort to build up.

The second point concerns the knowledge profile of the investment officers of banks. As we all know, a business organization is a collection of complex systems. Part of the health and future performance of the business is revealed by accounting figures and publicly available business news. A more complete set of skills is needed to get a more complete picture of the business firm under study.

This point is useful for us to understand why many investment funds do not perform too well. It is not that business organizations are impossible to understand, for we have seen the star performance of people like Warren Buffett. Perhaps, banks and financial firms should rethink the psychological and knowledge profile needed for fund management. In terms of the ability to understand a business firm better, a person with experience as a CEO or an angel investor is likely to do a better job than one who is skilled only in reading financial reports and digesting business news.[11]

CHAPTER 10

Counter-Cyclical Measures

In the Asian financial crisis a decade ago, a group of hedge funds sold Hong Kong stocks short. The proceeds were then converted into US dollars. The plan was to force the Hong Kong government to raise interest rates, which would result in a further fall of stock prices. The hedge funds would reap a huge profit from the stock market bet.

Alternatively, the government might yield under pressure by devaluating the currency, in which case the hedge funds would make a killing from the currency speculation.

The funds believed that Hong Kong, well-known for its free market and open economy, would do nothing to intervene in the market. But that was an unusual time; and unusual time called for unusual response. To the surprise of the speculators, the then Hong Kong Finance Secretary, Donald Tsang, used the war chest of the government to buy the stocks and restricted short selling. With these two strokes, the financial storm was basically over, and the hedge funds retreated to nurse their wounds.

Tsang's move earned him the wrath of the Nobel economics laureate Milton Friedman who called it insane.[1] Insane or not, the move was welcomed by investors. When the market recovered, the stocks were sold thus fattening the coffers of the Hong Kong government.

A decade after the Asian financial meltdown, the world is now facing the worst financial crisis since the Great Depression. The decade has provided time for economists and central bankers to reflect on Donald Tsang's move in 1998. Was it an act of insanity or economic wisdom? The answer is seen in the bailout of American Insurance Group, Citigroup and other financial institutions. Some call it a temporary nationalization. Perhaps it is better to call it smart investment on behalf of taxpayers.

A Core Idea of Keynesian Economics

Donald Tsang and his team of advisers creatively applied an idea of John Keynes, arguably the greatest economist of the last century. Keynes appreciated the productive capacity of capitalist dynamism, although this dynamism carries with it the dark power to cause havoc and chaos. This dualism of capitalism is manifested in the boom and bust cycles. Unlike Karl Marx who called for capitalism to be replaced by socialism, Keynes tried to fix it. He succeeded. Since the Great Depression, government interventions have time and again helped the economy to recover from recessions. It is wrong to say that Keynes is against free market; he is certainly against planned economy. He is fully aware of market failures. Market can regulate itself, but not all the time. It is like our human body, which can heal itself most of the time. We need medical treatment when we are seriously ill, or when we have a bad accident.

Keynes is most well-known for the macroeconomic policy of government spending to boost demand during recession by running budget deficits. There is general consensus among economists of different ideological hues that market mechanisms cannot be relied upon to restore stability during times of financial meltdown. Abandoning the gold standard has given governments the monetary flexibility to increase liquidity, and this flexibility should be used to full advantage to boost demand in times of recession.

The essence of Keynesian state intervention is the adoption of counter-cyclical measures to deal with economic downturns. The idea harks back to the Biblical story of the seven good years and seven bad years. The story provides us with a powerful tool for economic management. It can be encapsulated in one term — counter-cyclical measures. When inflation is raising its ugly head, tighten monetary and fiscal policies. In times of recession, do the opposite.

Asset Inflation and Deflation

It has been generally accepted that central banks should use monetary policy to manage inflation. Asset inflation is a more controversial issue. Some argue that central banks should raise interest rates too, while others argue this is not the concern of central banks. The issue is even more complicated when there is no threat of inflation then and in the near future. No central bankers want to be accused of causing a deflationary cycle.

Based on the spirit of Keynesian economics, governments should take measures to manage asset inflation in the same spirit as they manage consumer price index (CPI) inflation. There are nine possible combinations, namely, (1) CPI inflation and asset inflation; (2) CPI inflation and no asset inflation; (3) no CPI inflation and no asset inflation; (4) no CPI inflation but asset inflation; (5) CPI inflation and asset deflation; (6) CPI deflation and asset inflation; (7) CPI deflation and asset deflation; (8) no CPI inflation but asset deflation; and (9) CPI deflation and no asset inflation.

The easiest case to handle is when there is no CPI inflation and no asset inflation — the most ideal situation for any central banker. CPI inflation has been successfully managed with interest rate hikes, which also does not present any problem. So we can leave cases (1), (2) and (3) aside and move on.

There are a few ways to manage asset inflation. For stocks transaction, the government can increase stamp duty and (where applicable) capital gain tax. Loans for margin trading in stocks are to be restricted. Those governments who hold huge stakes in the stocks of their local companies (like China) will do well to sell the stocks in a planned and organized fashion. For transactions of residential units, stamp duties and down payments are to be increased. Additionally, the governments can announce their plans to release more land for residential buildings. Capital gain from sales of houses not occupied by owners is taxed more heavily than before. Governments should take the opposite action in times of asset deflation.

CPI inflation with asset deflation in the background is more difficult to handle. The government cannot afford to tighten the monetary policy to deal with the inflation for obvious reason. Reduction of general sales tax is a good way out. In the case of imported inflation due to oil price hike, reduction of petrol tax is certainly a sensible measure. Such situation illustrates to critics of government taxation the value of tax as a powerful tool in macroeconomic management.

Problems of Implementation

Principle is one thing. Implementation is another. We all know that interest rates should be increased to cope with inflation, but it is not easy to know when to do so and by how much. It is a difficult question of implementation that requires a team of highly competent experts working under the supervision of the central banker.

Implementing anti-cyclical measures to manage asset inflation and deflation is even more difficult. Which business firm is good enough for you to buy its stock? Bearish sentiments can last for months and months. When is the time for the state to step in to have the best picks? Unfortunately, there are very few people with the ability of Warren Buffett.

Bailouts are always a sensitive matter, especially when some firms are owned or run by people who are connected to the ruling party or government. In many countries, this can easily become another avenue for corruption. There is also the problem of moral hazard. It is conceivable that the task of bailouts is to be handled by an independent state institution other than the central bank. The integrity, competence and professionalism of the people there should be at least as stellar as those running the central banks.

Counter-cyclical measures, if skilfully and professionally exercised, will form an integral and indispensable element of a favourable business environment. It is just as important as the legal environment and physical infrastructure. As such, it is part and parcel of the competitive advantage that countries can offer to investors.

CHAPTER 11

Some Deeper Issues

The current financial tsunami originating from Wall Street provides us with an occasion to focus our minds on some deeper issues. If those in positions of power, policy-making and influence can sort out these issues, a bad thing may turn into a good thing.

To begin with, did the subprime mortgage defaults cause the meltdown? No. They only triggered it and exacerbated it as well. From an economist perspective, the financial crisis is essentially due to three types of imbalances. The first type of imbalance exists in the form of income disparity. Second is the imbalance in the form of current account deficit. Third is the financial sector imbalance that has dispersed and magnified risks for the global financial system.[1] We have looked at the third imbalance in previous chapters. We shall now go through the main points of the first two imbalances. We shall also touch on two other related topics — big government and information economy.

Economic Equity and Social Safety Net

Why do ordinary people have to take loans? Unlike businessmen and investors, they do not go into debt as part of the strategy to make more money. They do so because their income is insufficient to meet household expenses, to own a house and to send their children to college. Between 1980 and 2004 in the US, the average hourly wage in 2004 dollars hardly changed from the 1980 level of $15.68 per hour. In the same period, worker productivity increased by 68%.[2] Meanwhile, normal social life requires people to have a mobile phone. The list of normal expenses has become longer. Medicare has become much more expensive. A huge market has emerged for banks to take advantage of and credit card debt is a natural outcome. The subprime loans cater mainly to these lower income groups. They are more likely to be unable to service their house loans because of their low incomes.

The same may be said of student loans. The debt problem needs a fundamental solution. The income disparity of the people must be narrowed. It is in line with the ideal of economic justice and social equity.

The income disparity in China does not present an optimistic picture either. Moreover, in view of the lack of state investment in medical care and basic education, people have to save as much as they can. This explains why the saving rate in China has remained high. "This is not necessarily because the Chinese people are economically super-prudent, but because the insufficient socio-economic welfare system makes them feel insecure about healthcare, children's education, unexpected rainy days and eventual retirements."[3] Put differently, a government-sponsored safety net must be in place before we can expect any significant increase in private consumption in China.

We are still left with the problem of huge public debts and increasing budget deficits of the US administration.

It is too big a topic to be treated here. Suffice to say, the problem is political in nature and not resolvable by a purely economic solution.

Economic Realism and Political Parochialism

Theoretically, it is easy to devise a solution to deal with the current account imbalances of the US, European Union member states, China, Japan, the oil-rich countries, and others. Unlike the common parlance, the devil is not in the details but in the politics.

China is cash-rich, but it is badly in need of advanced technology to help it clean up the environment and to embark on the next level of economic development based on technology. The solution is pretty straightforward. Would China use some of its vast foreign reserves to buy the needed technology from the West? With a depressed market, China is in a good position to strike a good bargain. For China, this is far better than to see its dollars shrinking in real value over time. For the West, China represents one of the few markets which have the money to buy their advanced technologies. As long as it does not involve military technology, there is no valid political argument to block high-tech sales.

Another way to reduce the current account imbalance is for the West to allow sovereign wealth funds to buy their assets. The Middle East oil states, Singapore and China and other Asian countries have mountains of cash. In the past, they faced politically motivated opposition when they tried to acquire assets in the West. In spite of repeated assurances by the SWFs, Western governments still believed that SWFs were like the financial fifth columns of their governments. Luckily, this is changing. As you will read in a later chapter, Washington has introduced a rapid approval process for China's financial institutions to invest in the USA.

Big Government and Recession

Market economy has certainly proved its merits in generating growth and wealth. This has led to a body of knowledge and a community of scholars and politicians who advocate the ideology of big market and small government. This may be fine if market discipline really works well and when it does not, the consequences of market failures are not serious. Unfortunately, we have witnessed too many recessions and for some Latin American countries, even depressions during our lifetime. In fact, booms and busts are inseparable parts of credit-driven capitalist economy. Booms and busts can be likened to days and nights of monetary economy.

We are now experiencing the failure of self-regulatory mechanisms of free market. Except the ideological diehards, many are calling upon governments to do something drastic and fast to rescue the economy. Fortunately, one aspect of modern capitalism is that the role of government in the economy has increased radically both in size and scope. As Hyman Minsky observes, "The current much larger share of government in the advanced capitalist economies means that aggregate profits cannot fall to the low ratios to gross product that occurred in earlier times."[4] It may be added here that a big government must be run by a responsible and competent civil service whose loyalty is to the state and not to any party in power. It must not be a government well known for its expertise in oppressing the people. In the global competition for talents and investment, a new factor is entering the picture — competent and responsible *big* government.

Strange as it may sound, a free market economy can only work and survive with a strong and big government.

Reflections on Information Economy

At the height of the dot-com euphoria, we heard a powerful voice saying that the information economy was different. Dot-com companies were burning shareholders' money and bank loans to grow their market share. Asset valuation focused on market share rather than the ability to earn profit. We were told that we had entered the era of new economy with a different set of logics. This powerful voice overwhelmed the voice of sobriety which argued that the productivity due to IT could not mean that we could ignore the economic reality of making profits. The bursting of the bubble was good for the study of economics. We know that firms still need to make steady profits in order to survive.

However, the dot-com saga fails to drum into our head another idea, namely that firms must deliver value-added services and products to justify their income stream. Admittedly, it is sometimes difficult to tell what activity adds value to customers and society and which does not. Here a dose of commonsense and honesty is indispensable. Looking after babies is value-adding, whether the work is paid or not. The same may be said of voluntary work in the service of community.

The banking and financial industry is seen as a prototypical industry in the information economy. It deals with data and information, and uses computer as its workhorse. Here, brains are more valued than muscles. Such general observations do not raise the crucial question: in what way does it add value to the customers. More importantly, in what way does it add value to society?

Hedge funds make their money by betting on market trends. If they are lucky, they make lots of money for their investors. But, what is their contribution to society and economy? In past cases when they join hands to create a crisis as in the case of attack on the Hong Kong financial market in 1998, what is their contribution? They have probably used up hundreds of hours of computer time, transmitted millions of bytes through telephone lines. These are some mundane technical features of information economy. Cynics may be excused for saying that hedge funds give information economy a bad name. The may be right or they may be wrong. But what is relevant for us here is to note that information economy, just like the old economy, cannot ignore a fundamental principle of business economy and that is, they must deliver value to both their clients and society to justify their survival.

Two Opposed Ideas in the Mind at the Same Time

The discussion on the need of economic justice, social safety nets and big government may cause disquiet among those who believe in the virtues of free market and open economy. How can one reconcile politically the concept of free market with big government? How can one accept ideologically the idea that capitalism needs social safety nets to cushion the vagaries of economic turmoils?

A simple answer is that the real world is not a world built for the pleasure of theoretical purists and ideological fundamentalists.

The real world is the world for the pragmatists. They could be inspired by ideals. But they must learn to accept that gravitational force will always pull them back to earth. The Chinese are fond of referring to the famous discourse on cats by Deng Xiaoping, the former Chinese leader who initiated the economic reform in China. "A cat that catches mice is a good cat; it does not matter whether its colour is black or white." This advice is perhaps the best medicine for those addicted to ideological purity and theoretical beauty.

Perhaps we can supplement Deng's wise words with a piece of wisdom of Francis Scott Fitzgerald (1896–1940), an Irish-American novelist and short story writer. He observes that the test of a first-rate intelligence is the ability to hold two opposed ideas in the mind at the same time, and still retain the ability to function.

PART TWO

The East Asian Response

CHAPTER 12

The 1997 Asian Financial Crisis

The emerging economies especially China seem to be less affected by what is happening in the US. The following chapters will look at why Asian economies have been less affected by the global financial crisis thus far and some like Japan have managed to even go on a buying spree of American financial institutions. Is corporate governance the main reasons here? Or culture, management styles or even a state-led model? Did the Asian sovereign funds help to be the last line of defense against the excesses of the crisis? All these commonly-cited features of the so-called East Asian state-led model of development will be examined in this chapter. In this trend of thought, debates surrounding the hybrid Chinese model of capitalistic free marketplace and authoritarian political system will also be examined.

The crisis has also prompted some to turn to regulation as a panacea. Is East Asian-style state-led models with its characteristic governmental intervention and host of regulation the defense mechanism that protected East Asian economies from the crisis? Does this mark the rise of the Beijing consensus? If so, what then is the Beijing consensus? Is it a universally accepted model? Can it replace the Washington consensus? Or is there really no such thing as a Beijing consensus but really a modification and adaptation of existing global economic structure.

In the discussion of proposed solutions to the financial crisis, it is often pointed out that unilateralism is to be condemned, especially in the European case where non-coordination is often cited in comparison with the US's prompt and coordinated response in coming up with the US$700 billion bailout package. In the spirit of coordination versus unilateralism, this chapter will examine Asia's response. Is Asia yet another example of unilateralism action towards the crisis or is the US$80 billion Asian crisis fund the first instance of a coordinated East Asian response to the crisis?

Would this truly underpin the creation of an East Asian regional order that would eventually lead to instruments like an Asian Monetary Fund or currency swaps leading to a full-blown convertible regional currency? Is the Asian way of quiet diplomacy also applicable to their management of the global financial crisis? Is the preferred channel of bilateralism an alternative or hindrance to the East Asian response? Can Northeast Asian powers truly reconcile with each other to create a regional order that would eventually have an impact on the global financial system?

Is the much vaunted decoupling of Asian economies from the US ultimately proven by the financial crisis or to the contrary? Can East Asia create an insulated regional order or will this crisis prompt greater intra-regional coordination and a collective response in dealing with extra-regional state and non-state actors in the global economic and financial systems?

Background

Before the 1997 Asian economic crisis, the 21st century was touted as the Pacific century. East Asian economies before 1997 were enjoying high growth rates, some of which were double-digits. The real income of the Japanese increased four folds from 1960 to 1985 and it created an inspirational model for other East Asian countries to follow. Similarly, South Korea, Taiwan and Hong Kong saw the size of their economies doubling every eight years from 1960–1985.

Overall, these four economies together with the newly emerging economies, Malaysia, China, Thailand and Indonesia, were among the world's 13 most successful countries at raising real incomes from 1960–1990; between 1970–1990, the number of chronically poor people fell from 400 to 180 million in these economies.[1] In 1986, Vietnam began to follow China's example in freeing up its economy to market forces and achieved double-digit growth in the 1990s.

The success of pre-1997 East Asian economies were characterized by a few factors like high savings rate, hardworking citizens, anti-welfarism, emphasis on education, aggressive export policies, etc. These factors for economic growth in both Northeast and Southeast Asia were lumped together in the 1993 World Bank report, *The East Asian Miracle*, to serve as a form of inspiration for the bulk of the world's developing nations. Some examples will be provided here. In terms of savings rate, Taiwan's gross savings rate, for example, was around 35% of its Gross Domestic Product (GDP). Overall, Asia's high savings rate was over 30% of the value of its economic output thus creating one of the world's largest pools of capital.[2]

General Weaknesses of the East Asian Economies

The strength of the East Asian economies was tested by the 1997 Asian economic crisis. It started off with a rapid decline in the value of the Thai baht and thereafter it spread very quickly. 1997 saw major Asian currencies such as the Korean won and Indonesian rupiah plummeting very quickly. Before long, the whole region with the exception of China and Taiwan plunged into an economic crisis.

Besides their currencies, the manufacturing output of the Asian economies also declined. For example, the Republic of Korea experienced a 25% fall in the terms of trade of its manufactured exports between 1995 and 1997 due to the Asian economic crisis accompanied by a glut in electronics components in the world market. In Southeast Asia, even the brightest rising stars in manufacturing like Malaysia saw her exports fell by 7%.[3]

In 1997, even the most resilient of the Asian economies began to falter. This was caused by many factors such as a global electronics glut, the weakness of the US economy, the stagnant economy in Japan, the September 11 terrorist attacks, the Information Technology (IT) bubble burst, the stagnant Japanese economy and the persisting fallouts of the 1997 Asian economic crisis. Even China's exports, long thought to be immune to global contagion, caught the chill and registered a drop by 0.6% in June.[4] In US dollar terms, Taiwan's exports fell 1.12% in 2000, from a forecasted growth of 5.68% in January.[5] In June 2001 alone, Taiwan's exports plunged by 16.6%.[6]

Why Did It Happen?

The important factor that contributed to the economic crisis was the process of economic globalization that allowed rapid financial flows which is volatile, unstable, irrational and tends to be uncontrollable, to take place in the market. The openness and closeness of Asian markets to these capital flows, the volatility of the global financial markets as well as the way the capital is utilized affected the state of Asian economies. This market volatility, together with cultural values influencing the way Asians do business, created the financial crisis. For example in Thailand, capital inflows were misallocated to borrowers and this was associated with cultural values such as the way Thais do business. In another example, loans in Korea exceeded 60% of Korea's total external liabilities.

The misallocation of funds in these two cases arises partly from Asia's Confucianist traditions, for example *guanxi*, which encourage cronyism, nepotism, patron-client networks and corruption. In Southeast Asia, these values are propagated by overseas Chinese networks while Northeast Asia shares similar cultural roots with China, resulting in paternalistic developmental states in Japan and Korea. Thus, when the global financial markets became volatile and overextended banks tried to recall these bad loans, the two combined factors create a crisis.

The misallocation of funds clearly indicated the need for good economic governance for capital inflows to be used productively. In this perspective, the financial crisis creates a good opportunity for Asian countries to reform their economic sectors and install structures for good governance. Thus, good economic governance has become a factor for consideration when the International Monetary Fund (IMF) dispenses funds to aid the Asian countries that were struck by the financial crisis.

The 1997 Asian financial crisis indicated that East Asia still needed corporate governance and rules formulated by global institutions including those in the US and Japan's initiative for an Asian Monetary Fund (AMF). Good governance connotes certain values like greater participation, transparency, openness and accountability that will help to deepen or democratize domestic democracy in East Asian countries. Greater participation refers to the empowerment of Non-Governmental Organizations (NGOs), introduction of greater local autonomy and reduction of state power. As a result, NGOs and local powers rise up to challenge the old cultural values of the state, pressuring it to have a greater accountability. These values are incorporated in good governance for East Asia.

For example, the civil society and academics in Thailand could stimulate public awareness for good governance in private and public spheres as the power of NGOs is proportionately increased by globalization. Localization can help weaken the state's cultural hegemony by making people more aware of the economic problems around them and through the media, curb excesses created at the local level.

Questions emerge quickly about the need to address Asian economic policies that hitherto had been aggressive export policies, dependence on mainly the US and Japanese markets as well as emphasis on high-tech sectors in a bid to leap-frog several stages in economic development. The vulnerability of dependence on export markets, especially in the high-tech sectors, was revealed when global semiconductor sales dropped by 20% in May compared with 2000.[7]

The impact of the global decline on East Asia's exports and economic growth in the early 21st century has been catastrophic. For example between January 2000 and July 2001, the price of standard 64-megabyte DRAM chips dropped by 90% from 8.93 dollars to just 0.92 dollars.[8] In the countries that had invested most in electronics production — Malaysia, Korea and Taiwan — exports contracted sharply in the second quarter. Countries in the region have over-invested in electronics manufacturing thus leaving them highly vulnerable to shifts in technological evolution.

Other than the manufacturing sector, another problem that is just as deep-seated is found in the financial sector. In view of the many quarters, the biggest flaw amongst the East Asian economies, as pointed out by even the ardent optimists of East Asian prospects, is the inability to develop transparent and objective public institutions as well as systems of accountability in private companies, hence leading to widespread corruption and bad accounting in the East Asian economies. For example, the liberalization of financial services in the countries was not accompanied by an increase in effective governmental regulations and accountable corporate governance. Since the 1997 Asian economic crisis was considered to be a financial one and the genesis of many East Asian problems, a brief background on the 1997 Asian economic crisis is further discussed here.

The most affected victims of the 1997 Asian financial crisis were Indonesia, South Korea, Malaysia and Thailand. Each country have different attributes and their initial troubles of 1997 were also different. However, what they had in common was that all four countries experienced very fast economic growth and even faster financial growth, without acquiring the bureaucratic apparatus needed to deter companies from lying to creditors and shareholders, to prevent banks from lending recklessly while borrowing abroad just as recklessly, and to ensure fairness in stocks markets. In other words, there was a lack of effective and clean corporations, and economic governance.

In some of these countries, the government or individual leaders and their families were deeply implicated in all that was going on: an explosion of bank credit to favoured companies and individuals well beyond their capacity to repay the loans; an explosion of real estate and stock-market speculation, fed by more wildly imprudent bank loans; and an explosion of corporate and bank debt to foreign banks and investors. Summarily, one of the key problems was thus the failure of the ex-tiger economies to adequately reform their banking sectors. This has severely impeded corporate debt restructuring and the re-entry of international investors.

Besides the problems in the manufacturing and financial sectors, the other big problem in East Asia was its over-dependence on Japan and the US for growth. The US market has been volatile with her economy buoyant at the height of the Internet bubble and then crashing down hard, bringing all East Asian economies along with it. It then went up substantially with the completion of the shakeout and growth in demand for semiconductors. The rest of the East Asian economies then followed it down in a spiral spin with the occurence of the September 11 terrorist attacks.

Japan, the other engine of growth in East Asia, had been mired in an on-off recession when its bubble economy collapsed in 1989–1990. Her banks were previously paralyzed by the double blows of the collapse in land prices and Japanese shares. While their own capital base lost just about half its value, many of their assets (i.e. loans outstanding) also became valueless when clients who had borrowed to buy land and shares at the top of the market could neither repay their loans nor even keep up interest payments.

Only the liabilities of the banks (i.e. deposits) did not decline. The banks therefore had to cut their lending, especially to smaller firms. As the lack of credit started to strangle the economy, consumer demand collapsed and many firms and shops saw their sales decline by a third or more between 1990 and 1997.[9] The banks were in so much trouble that in early 1998, even Sumitomo Bank had to offer a 10% coupon to sell its dollar-denominated preferred shares on the New York market.[10] Many corporations were in trouble, especially if they had borrowed money to buy real estate or other corporate shares during the boom years. Japan had to battle with a stock market at 37% of the 1989 peak, and Tokyo's real estates were on offer for one-third of the prices in 1989.[11] Its 5% unemployment rate is also the highest in post-war era.

In all, the combined effect of a glut in global electronics supply, bad financial corporate governance, decline in the US engines of growth like IT and weaknesses in the US and Japanese economies had affected the East Asian economies adversely in 1997. Though East Asian countries collectively experienced similar boom perks at the peak of the strength of East Asian economies and faced similar problems at the height of the Asian economic crisis, it is increasingly apparent that the two regions of Northeast and Southeast Asian economies were beginning to evolve separately shaped by both boom and lean time environmental factors and their different attributes.

Rocket-fast growth in Southeast Asia was affected by the Asian financial crisis. It devastated the industrial structure of Asian economies and created difficulties for export-dependent Asian economies. Below is a snapshot of what happened in aftermath of the 1997 crisis.

Thailand was the first country to be hit by the Asian economic crisis in 1997. In the aftermath, Thailand's financial system was fragile and there was pressure for her monetary policies to ease. Thailand suffered from the problem of high public debts. Partly because of public dissatisfaction with reforms implemented by IMF, Chuan Leekpai was voted out of power and Thaksin replaced him as Prime Minister. Due to the protracted hardship after 1997, there was constant pressure by some quarters to apply the Malaysian Mahathir-style currency control to stabilize the economy. However, the Thais largely followed IMF reforms.

In the aftermath of the 1997 crisis, Malaysia experienced a contraction of its economy with weak domestic demand. Fiscal policies remained the number one response to the weakening global economy. The Malaysian economy was also fortunate to have commodity prices holding up their economy despite the global downturn. To encourage more spending, the government cut income tax for the individual and increased the pay for civil servants. However, the weakness in the Malaysian economy remained — debts incurred by statutory boards known as Non-Public Enterprises (NPEs) such as Tenaga. The government experienced a budget deficit due to the need to bail out some of these companies. Many economists also wondered how long Malaysia could continue with its prime-pumping and propping up the ringgit.

It was mostly negative news in Indonesia. The country was plagued by the volatility of the rupiah especially after the 1997 Asian financial crisis.

Certain segments of the Indonesian economy did go rather well. For example, the cigarette and cement industries went up, indicating that the fundamental Indonesian economy held up. Cement use for minor construction work like building balconies for houses for example went up. These factors reflected the early gradual recovery after 1997. In the same vein, the number of cars sold in Indonesia increased. Consumption spending on the most basic levels in Indonesia also went up. Indonesia, like many other Southeast Asian countries, relied on the rural sector and domestic demand, both of which are vulnerable to the global economic climate.

CHAPTER 13

Ten Years After the Asian Financial Crisis — Positive Lessons Learned

When Thailand devalued its currency on 2 July 1997, it caused the financial crisis that engulfed nearly the entire Southeast Asian region with one casualty in Northeast Asia (South Korea). The crisis-affected Southeast Asian countries stabilized themselves in the aftermath but never really regained the dazzling growth of the mid-1990s.

Outside economics, many major Southeast Asian countries remained politically unstable in the aftermath of 1997. This includes a military coup and political violence in the South in Thailand in 2006; a Communist insurgency in Philippines; Indonesia slowly recovered from the collapse of the Suharto government and fallout from terrorism; and the Bali bombings in 2002.

In contrast, the only real victim of the crisis in Northeast Asia, South Korea, recovered and grew stronger. "Korea's economic policy has become more consistent during the last 10 years," said Lee Jang Yung, the assistant governor at the South Korean government's Financial Supervisory Service. "Its financial system has become stronger and sound." Within two years, South Korea bounced back; after a 7% economic contraction in 1998, it regained growth in 1999 following an aggressive restructuring programme. The crisis forced South Korea to open up its economy, resulting in an inflow of FDI amounting to $102 billion from 1998 to 2006, or 80% of the country's inbound investments since 1962.

Southeast Asia fell behind the European Union (EU) and the North American Free Trade Agreement (NAFTA) in regional economic integration and was severely dependent on a genuine and robust reconciliation between Japan and China to have an integrated future. Due to such factors, Southeast Asian countries, with the exception of Vietnam, were no longer the real stars of economic growth in East Asia. The baton is now passed over to the growth rates of 9–11% in Asia's three current stars: China, India and the only Southeast Asian candidate, Vietnam.

Vietnam, which once rivaled Laos and Papua New Guinea in poverty surpassed Thailand in annual cement consumption while China became the world's leading steel producer and India became a global leader in computer software development and other outsourcing sectors, and recorded double-digit growth in manufacturing as well. In Northeast Asia, a sign of Chinese economic power is that, while many Southeast Asian countries used to ship electronics and other goods directly to the US, today they tend to ship components to China, where they are assembled and shipped to American ports.

At the height of the crisis, China remained a bastion of stability and despite losing its export competitiveness as other countries' currencies fell; China's decision not to devalue its renminbi (yuan) played a critical role in stabilizing the economy. "In a responsible manner, the

Chinese government committed not to depreciate the currency and took a series of active measures to help those countries recover from the crisis." Wu Xiaoling, the vice-governor of China's central bank, said at the *Asian Financial Crisis 10th Anniversary Forum* held in Beijing.

One big beneficiary of Chinese economic power was Hong Kong. After Hong Kong returned to China's sovereignty on 1 July 1997, the Asian financial crisis struck the next day, spiraling Hong Kong into its longest recession in history before it was rescued by Chinese economic power, inducing Hong Kong citizens to appreciate their dependence on China — perhaps for the first time since colonization. Backed by Beijing, Hong Kong's first Chinese financial secretary Donald Tsang spearheaded a HK$120 billion (S$23 billion) strategy to fend off speculative attacks on the city's stock and currency markets which could have crashed the market by punting on the Hong Kong currency and bargain-priced shares.

China also actively took part in the IMF aid programme, offering $4 billion to the Asian countries affected. The Chinese government also realized that the crisis elsewhere in the region was caused by a lack of transparency in financial systems and undertook its structural reforms to avoid falling into the trap that the other Asian economies fell into. The solutions by the Chinese government were quick and decisive.

In 1998, the government injected 270 billion yuan into state-owned commercial banks and peeled off 1.4 trillion yuan worth of bad loans for them and then quickly implemented reforms. State-owned giants including China Industrial and Commercial Bank, China Construction Bank, China Bank, China Communication Bank and some others successfully listed on Chinese and overseas stock markets, which greatly increased their transparency boosted by supervision based on international standard accounting and auditing rules improved governance as well.

In the years following the Asian financial crisis in 1997, countries in East Asia had institutionally practiced prudent fiscal policies, keeping budget deficits relatively small, managing debt burdens effectively, and limiting exposure to liabilities as their recipes to getting out of the crisis. Many had good progress and even remarkable successes in such policies. Many had also ridden on the backs of export-oriented dynamism through exports to industrial countries, growing intra-regional trade and increasingly, consumer demand.

The Positives

The results of such policies in general were that banks became liquid and solvent, inflation was low, exchange rates were less volatile, and economic activity increased. Three years after the crisis, the UN had a favorable assessment of East Asia's recovery, characterizing it as occurring in an "environment of lower inflation, enhanced business and consumer confidence, and an increasing flow in foreign investment in the region" and "in fact, these factors, combined with the economic restructuring efforts supported by fiscal stimuli and buoyant export." Even the World Bank admitted in a 2007 report that a decade after Asia's financial crisis rocked the region in 1997–1998, East Asian economies are institutionally stronger, much wealthier and have a larger global role than before.[1]

There were successes in fiscal policies; fiscalization comprising of both the financing of bank bailouts and restructuring, as well as other public sector expenditures to mitigate the impact of the financial crisis and kick start the economy. Such features were the age-old state models, which have characterized the East Asian developmental model for most of the post-war years. In other words, state-led institutional reforms on managing and tweaking the economy for fastest possible growth was re-applied effectively with a vengeance in post-crisis East Asia.

Fiscal discipline was a common and preferred antidote by many East Asian states. An example of effective post-1997 macro fiscal policies can be found in Thailand, the widely seen originator of the crisis pandemic. Thailand maintained fiscal discipline regarding on-budget expenditures and kept its central government budget deficit below 3% of GDP every year since the crisis except when it reached 3.3% in 1999, and the budget deficit for 2002 was only 1.4% of GDP.[2]

Thailand's management of its long-term debt had been prudent. While total public debt shot up from 14.5% of GDP in 1996 to 57.9% of GDP in 2001, this debt ratio has declined and did not threaten Thailand's overall fiscal soundness.[3] In order to jump-start the economy, Thai government debt increased more than seven-fold from its 5.2% debt ratio in 1996 to 38.8% in 2000, as public expenditures were made to support financial institutions and expansionary fiscal policies were pursued to stimulate economic recovery.[4]

Indonesia had also been quite prudent with on-budget expenditures since the crisis, keeping its budget deficit to less than 3% of GDP every year except 2001, when the debt ratio reached a peak of 3.7%.[5] Like Thailand, the Indonesian governments used state financial instruments to bail out and provide guarantees for the countries' financial institutions. Indonesia issued approximately Rp 740 trillion in government bonds ($87 billion at the current exchange rate), equal to two-thirds of 1999 GDP (when most of the bonds were issued) to cover a number of liabilities incurred during the financial crisis: compensation to Bank Indonesia for liquidity and solvency support to struggling banks; compensation to banks that assumed liabilities of banks closed by the government; and recapitalization of undercapitalized banks that remained open.

CHAPTER 14

Ten Years After the Asian Financial Crisis — Negative Lessons Learned

The Negatives

As late as 2005, some in the business sector continued to warn against complacency and urge institutional reforms to continue region-wide. Then Citibank chairman William R. Rhodes Friday advised Asian economies to resume efforts on reforming the financial sector, warning that the slow pace of reforms may trigger another financial crisis in the region: "In many cases, the high levels of liquidity and lower non-performing loans have led to a slowing of reforms. And in this sense, I am not so sure whether the 1997 Asian financial crisis will not occur again."[1]

The reasons for the warnings given were found in the fact that the immediate panic and anxiety for reforms in the aftermath of the crisis was replaced by the complacency of calm, so non-performing loans growing on the balance sheets of banks and future bailouts might be necessary. The weakness of post-crisis institutional reforms was also buttressed by economic recoveries that have also been consumption rather than production-led, and in some cases supported by government stimulus packages, the combination of which could result in further financial sector stress due to consumer over-crediting and unsustainable household debt levels, as well as greater fiscal stress because of lower tax revenue and unsustainable public sector expenditure levels.

Relying solely on the state to jump-start the economy through the use of government funds could lead to both a large revenue shortfall, as well as increased public expenditures and accentuate the economic downturn's effect on the poor through higher taxation. Both countries deemed as most vulnerable to another crisis, Thailand and Indonesia, had a lingering problem of a large revenue shortfall coupled with increased public expenditures should the country suffer another significant and sustained slowdown in economic growth.

In addition, the guarantees given by governments like the Thais had the potential of unrealizability given their blanket nature. The largest documented government liability was the blanket guarantee introduced by Thailand in 1997 of all depositors and most creditors of domestic financial institutions. At the end of 2002, this guarantee covered liabilities that were slightly larger than total GDP and, while it was extremely unlikely that the blanket guarantee would be realized in its entirety, it was nonetheless a potentially large cost to the government should the financial sector experience another crisis.

Indonesia's blanket guarantee was equally staggering to stave off the initial impact of the crisis. The largest documented government contingent liability was the blanket guarantee provided by Presidential Decree No. 26 of January 1998, covering both domestic and foreign currency claims of all bank depositors and creditors except the holders of subordinated debt. At the end of 2002, this guarantee covered liabilities that were approximately half of the total GDP.[2] This was a potentially large cost to the government should the financial sector experience another crisis.

In Indonesia especially, the cost of liquidating government-owned banks that were non-performing or on an artificial lease of life buoyed by government funding was still an unknown, given the lower than preferred levels of transparency in Indonesia. Transparency was also another factor in the inability to assess Indonesia's governmental liabilities in the near future. While it had given guarantees and bailed out national banks, the state had other existing liabilities on the accounting sheet which had not been transparently tallied with the figures the country had spent to bail out of the 1997 financial crisis.

Before the Asian financial crisis in 1997, Indonesia was heralded by the World Bank as a prime example of a successful developing country notwithstanding its governance by a strong authoritarian military government. Before 1997, Indonesia achieved rapid economic development as one of the high performance dynamic ASEAN economies. This is only to be devastated by the Asian financial crisis which destabilized its economy, social and political structure. Since 2003, the Indonesian economy has gradually recovered, but many structural problems remain, such as high levels of unemployment and relatively low levels of foreign direct investment.

The biggest institutional weakness of regional economies was the vulnerability to large external shock which some commentators have given examples of slow-down in Chinese economic growth, political upheavals or US economic slowdown triggering off another round of crisis. Other factors may include a hardened protectionist stance by the US and further dislocation in the Middle East or the spike in oil prices. It could also be in the form of slow revival of the Japanese economy, to higher prices for oil or a loss of business and consumer confidence. East Asia should not discount the fact of such events happening.

Some advocated new ways of thinking to buffer against such eventualities or surprises. For example, tapping strongly into the flow of Asian savings into bank deposits to either let bank deposits migrate to mutual funds or compel bank deposits to go from low demand loans to funding enterprises via venture capital, mezzanine finance or private equity. Other ways include greater transparency and releasing more information so that surprises can be minimized and internal rot seen more transparently before it develops into an incurable cancer. Information was vital. For example, there was scant public information regarding unfunded government pension liabilities in Thailand and how this was spent, its volume and usability as a buffer fund against global financial crises triggers could be better explored with greater transparency.

This might also help in the social dimensions of the crisis learnt from the 1997 crisis: the crisis vividly showed the inadequacies in providing social protection to the most vulnerable groups of society: the poor, the infirmed, the elderly, the sick and the children. East Asian countries had to devise ways to prevent another domino fall of political leaders across the region due to social instability that arose out of the last crisis.

A more macro-solution suggested was establishing a common currency in the Asian economic bloc with a pan-Asian regulator of last resort which functions as a coordinator that will facilitate a common standard and sharing financial intelligence which will propel the growth of the Asian financial market. Moreover, East Asian governments' international reserves which can be put to better use and more flexible exchange rates would insulate the economies of developing Asia from imported cost push inflation from factors like higher oil prices, dampen increases in local interest rates, and contribute to alleviating global macroeconomic imbalances.

Finally, the less popular but more radical strategy was epitomized by Malaysia through its prime-pumping and currency control strategies. Malaysia seemed to head the pack when it comes to restricting the open outlook of Asian economies. In the financial front, many Southeast Asian countries were looking at Malaysia for answers as its restrictive ringgit control policies have worked so far in preventing the country from plunging into an economic crisis and its closed-door policies have prevented foreign penetration of IMF-obedient countries. Although criticized by many, it has worked for Malaysia thus far. This strategy is likely to remain unpopular with other East Asian economies because of its inclusive nature and its perceived lesser ability to take advantage of a global rebound due to its sheltering of the currency and some industries from competition.

CHAPTER 15

Deconstructing
the State-led Model

When one thinks of the archetypal early example of East Asian style economic regulation, the pioneering model of Japan immediately comes to mind. Historically, during the formative years of statehood, Japan did not place top priority on the individual maximization of self-interest of private enterprises through competition. Japan's Meiji roots in modern industrialization and commerce arose from the need to build up a wealthy nation and strong army (*fukoku kyohei*) to fend off potential Western colonizers.

As a result, companies organized themselves to form *zaibatsus* or business cartels (e.g. Mitsui) for the national interest of speeding up industrialization and competing in a more effective manner with more advanced Western companies. *Zaibatsu* basically acted like the old guilds as a form of private sector regulator of competition. Through strength in numbers, they dominated industries and manipulated pricing and demand to their advantage. These companies amassed tremendous profits through these illiberal means that curtailed free competition. The government benefited from this arrangement too as it could tap on these *zaibatsus'* fortunes for nation-building efforts.

After the American Occupation of Japan (1945–1952), some of these private sector groups managed to regroup themselves with government help for the priority of rebuilding the country. They became the *keiretsu* groupings that are companies within the same industry that forms strategic partnerships by allowing cross-shareholdings. Sometimes, a bank is at the centre of this grouping and it might purchase some shares of associated companies. The inclusion of banks in *keiretsus* resulted in the heavy reliance of Japanese companies on capital borrowed from their affiliated *keiretsu* banks rather than their own paid-in capital.

During times of economic difficulties, associated companies within the groupings help each other out through the voluntary absorption of other member companies' retrenched employees. It is also not unusual for the banks to send in some directors to member companies in difficulties to help them secure more loans as part of the group's obligations. These activities shelter some member companies against strong competition and economic downturns in the liberal free market. An example is Fujitsu that had received cheap loans on demand from affiliated banks.[1] Such companies were able to come about through purchasing agreements and cooperation with other private firms within their business groups.

Keiretsu were formed with the blessings of the bureaucracy and therefore continued to maintain close relationships with the bureaucracy. They formed strategic partnerships by allowing cross-shareholdings. Sometimes, a bank would be at the centre of this grouping and it might purchase shares of associated companies. A typical group includes a big bank, several industrial firms and a general trading company. The inclusion of the bank results in heavy reliance of Japanese companies on capital borrowed from banks rather than their own paid-in capital.

During times of economic difficulties, associated companies within the groupings would help each other out through voluntary absorption of other member companies' retrenched employees or other means. It is important to note that *keiretsu* groupings are mainly private sector-driven. As such, even after the ending of state monopolies and deregulation of an industry, *keiretsu* can still function without violating deregulatory measures. They do not infringe on deregulation as the government bureaucracy does not regulate them in an official manner like a state monopoly. However, they do maintain close links with the bureaucracy on an unofficial basis.

Governmental help restored an intimate working relationship between the private sector and the government. This intimate working relationship was also made possible through appointment of former government bureaucrats as advisors or senior management of MNCs. This process is known as *amakudari* or 'descent from heaven'. In the bumper year of 1992, 314 bureaucrats retired to join the telecommunication, construction and finance sectors.[2]

In addition, many of the administrative and business elites drawn from the elite universities create an old boys' network. The University of Tokyo classmates in and out of the government bureaucracy keep in touch with each other, and one reason private businesses are happy to recruit them is the cultivation of good relations and contact with government. Since they emerged from the same institutions, the worldviews and mindsets would be more similar and this was what the elites were hoping for. As a result, these groupings have their own insiders within the ministries. It is also not unusual for the banks to send in some directors to borrowing companies in difficulties as part of the group's obligations.

But the Japanese model went against liberal economic philosophy that was dominant in the US, especially in an age of globalization. Diana Coyle argued that globalization is the ability to move investments from country to country, into developing country and most important of all, it is autonomous in character. The autonomy of movement of investments brought about by globalization is not elaborated upon by Coyle in the same chapter. The 'autonomy of investments' also referred to the freedom of companies that control the investments and finances to move their money anywhere in the world in accordance with their choice and their view on the profitability of different markets around the world.

It is this feature that links globalization with deregulation, privatization and competition. We will explain why. The autonomy of investments means that worldwide investments are guided now by profitability, free of government bureaucratic control. Its goal is making money and not nationalism or nation-building for example. In such a system, the state would have to provide incentives for companies to invest in their country.

The autonomous nature of investments also confirmed Maurice Estabrooks' arguments that "traders, speculators and institutions have much more power than most governments especially when they work together" when there is money to be made.[3] The roots of capitalism arose from the private enterprise and the individual/companies' self-interest in seeking profits for themselves. As such, the motivation of companies in the world capitalist sector was overwhelmingly in control of companies and individuals, not governments that are not business entities to begin with.

This was because deregulation has ended government bureaucratic control over the industry. The privatization process that followed then transferred the fate of the industry from the government monopoly to the private sector. As the main motivation for the capitalist private sector was seeking profits, this has resulted in the autonomous nature of the private sector investments.

The scope of privatization included more than the entities of traders, speculators and institutions. Other entities like consumers, trade unions, banks and other organizations not related to the government also contribute to the market forces at work. As observed in the US liberal model, it is this plurality of forces at work that will sort out the workings of the market, and the mechanics of demand and supply in the economy as a whole. Driven by self-interest in the form of money, these entities are able to overcome government bureaucratic regulations. Even the powerful bureaucracy in the highly controlled and regulated Soviet economy cited by Milton Friedman is unable to stop private enterprises from making profits when they see their chances.

A Changed Environment

True enough, the Japanese model began to falter. In Japan, as the bureaucracy had been responsible for fast growth for most of the post-war years, some groups within the bureaucracy felt that it was legitimate for the bureaucracy to carry on with its regulatory role. Partly through this tight regulatory system, Japan quickly rose to become an advanced nation and the world's second largest economy.

With this sparkling result, the bureaucracy felt that it rightfully earned the legitimacy to continue with its regulatory role in Japan's industries. However, it became increasingly difficult to justify regulations. There were several main reasons why Japan gradually gave way to deregulation. They included changed bureaucratic legal wrangling, international commitment to deregulation, the benefits of the US liberal model in the IT industry, *gaiatsu* or foreign pressure and globalization.

If the 1960s was characterized by fast growth, the 1970s was characterized by Japan's trade frictions with its trading partners. In the 1970s, the sharp increase of Japan's exports of industrial products to the US and Europe began to cause international friction and this cumulated to the 1971 announcement that US would end the convertibility of the dollar into gold. In December 1971, Japan revalued the yen from 360 yen against the US dollar, which had been maintained for 22 years, to 308 yen and, in February 1973, Japan adopted a floating exchange-rate system.[4]

Subsequently in the 1980s, the trade imbalance with advanced industrial nations expanded because of the yen's appreciation. Eventually, Japan's trading partners decided to confront the frictions head-on. On 22 September 1985, finance ministers from the world's five largest economies — the US, Japan, West Germany, France and the UK — announced the Plaza Accord at the New York hotel. By this accord, Japan promised a looser monetary policy and a range of financial-sector reforms. By the end of 1987, the dollar had fallen by 54% against the yen from its peak in February 1985.[5]

Due to a sudden increase in the Japanese yen's exchange rate with the dollar, Japanese goods' competitiveness in pricing suddenly dramatically declined and was subjected to tough competition from other emerging East Asian countries with lower cost structures. This resulted in a large-scale capital outflow to South Korea, Taiwan, Hong Kong and subsequently to ASEAN. Japanese production costs had become too costly and the outflow of capital soon created highly competitive tiger economies that began to compete with Japan. They were smaller and nimbler than Japan's formerly formidable bureaucratically-planned economy.

Domestically in Japan, excessive restrictions that had intimidated foreign investors hurt the vital parts of the economy. For example, if a private-sector banking institution started a branch bank in a local area, it had to get the authorization from Ministry of Finance (MOF). Such excessive regulations need to be pared down to encourage foreign players to come into the Japanese market and create greater competitive pressures.

In the case of the *keiretsu*, resources from group members that were performing badly were not freed up to the rest of the economy because of three reasons. Firstly, the willingness of the member bank to lend money to member companies at low interest rates keeps the bad performing member companies in business. There might have also been a vicious cycle of banks lending these member companies money to keep them going because, in the event that they go bankrupt, the bank was not able to recover any of its principal sum back.

This prevented valuable financial resources from re-circulating back into the economy. Such bad loans may even have reverberations on other industries like the banking sector. Secondly, due to the willingness to absorb excess labour from each other, human resources from the less able members of the group are kept within the group and not freed up for more efficient use in the economy. In this manner, such human resources in the less competitive sectors are trapped doing peripheral jobs in other member companies just to protect employment.

At a macro-level, the problem plaguing Japan was that elite bureaucrats imposed their own sense of national aims on both corporate managers and consumers, weak industries were protected, rising industries were encouraged, and all sectors of the economy were directed to assure full employment. These policies prevented fast and effective deregulation from taking place. Administrative directions that were used to achieved this, once successful, are now being abandoned gradually in Japan in exchange for deregulation and free competition.

Full employment was always the overriding purpose of Japan's very particular version of controlled capitalism. Though best known for its protracted resistance to the globalization of Japan's own economy, while exporting hugely — its core was always a pervasive system of internal controls. Thus, in Japan and eventually Korea and other East Asian countries, one way of controlling capitalism and at the same time foster economic growth was to give the government the role to force-feed and guide their fastest possible growth.

This form of developmental capitalism was privately owned but subsidized, assisted and closely directed by powerful economic ministries and governmental agencies.

This form of economic development had been discredited as overly dominant control over the economy by the government had led to the inability to free the creative energies (Schumpeter's Creative destruction theory) and to inflexibility in the economy to respond to market needs as seen in the failure of Japan's ICT revolution.

CHAPTER 16

Reforming the State-led Model

Japanese Reforms

Augmented by the US surge in IT and New Economy features, there were calls for reform features that include more transparency, lesser government controls, greater competition including foreign competition, etc. These were the subjects of IMF conditions imposed on Korea, Thailand and Indonesia in exchange for monetary aid in the aftermath of the 1997 Asian financial crisis. These aims are also promoted by the WTO.

Consequently, because of such global and regional trends towards liberalization, globalization and decentralization as well as problems of competing in the global economy, Japan started to reform its economic bureaucracies to trim it further and reduce their powers. But resistance was strong and Japanese politicians demonstrated little effectiveness in this area as the mandarins in the bureaucracy held their grounds. This changed with the election of the highly popular former Prime Minister Junichiro Koizumi who assumed power on the platform of reforms starting from the postal savings and postal workers sector and battled vested interests including the bureaucracy.

Chinese Reforms

If reforms for Japan come with political battles with the bureaucracy, reforms in China are equally difficult. Liberalization and deregulation of the agricultural, banking or state-owned enterprises (SOEs) sectors have potential destabilizing effects on China. China's experiment in the reform of its policy regime would be the most interesting in East Asia. Its main challenge was to reconcile a socialist political system with a market economy.

The government would have to justify to the people as the Chinese people adjust to an emerging gap between the well-off and the poor or as the difference between the western provinces and the wealthy eastern coastal cities widens. The challenge to incorporate socialist thinking and the need to accommodate the Chinese entrepreneurial spirit was perhaps seen in the latest move by the Chinese Communist Party (CCP) to include bourgeoisie capitalists into their folds. Many of these new members saw CCP as a way to get better connections and get rich faster rather than political orthodoxy.

WTO created new policy challenges for China. Chinese scholars started off with the perception that WTO membership would only benefit China. However, in the rush to join WTO, China agreed to many terms imposed under WTO. It would have to steer gingerly through the course of balancing the interests of her

SOEs and the need to open up to foreign competition. The old subsidy system and protectionist measures and policy regime for her SOEs would have to change. At the current moment, China is 60% private sector and 40% SOE.[1]

The need for reforms in SOE was compounded by the problem that China had a weak financial sector. To the Chinese government, there were, however, also benefits of joining the WTO. For example, after joining the WTO, they can then point to WTO obligations and the competition that WTO will bring to China as an excuse to reform the economy of China, especially in the SOE sector.

Korean Reforms

The Korean government concluded its capital market development scheme in 2007, featuring the creation of investment banks that are globally-competitive to spearhead the growth of the capital markets by offering innovative financial products complementary to the needs of corporations and investors. The challenge remains with the sustainability of this bold, vibrant and welcomed reforms with the outbreak of the US subprime mortgage crisis in July 2007.

With the outbreak of the subprime crisis and its evolution into a global financial crisis, Korean observers, commentators, business analysts and scholars began to be wary of what it calls the US "free lunch model" arising from the weaknesses of the Wall Street model. This prompted Korea to initiate a rethink of its policy, especially since the post-2008 crisis highlights the importance of a new regulatory regime and framework to keep up with the speed and complications of new financial products that are difficult to understand. Several suggestions have been forwarded by Korean scholars to avoid a US-style financial meltdown.

These include treating credit agencies and ratings with caution and not use their information as foundations for building new businesses, manage risks or issue loans. Secondly, requiring banks to be more transparent and have higher levels of disclosure of their business transactions and activities, in the process fostering market discipline and curbing the excesses or financial innovation. Thirdly, to have greater channels of communications between parent holding companies and their subsidiaries with regards to coordination of activities, pool of resources, repackaging of assets and monitoring risks.

Fourthly, to create a culture of integrity, trust, openness and honesty and, lastly, to devise a more advanced capital regulation system for financial investment companies that will manage new products to prepare for a new financial environment and to buffer against any unexpected, externally caused losses in business without the need for financial help from the state or the central bank.

In Korea, the Act on the Capital Market and Financial Investment Business (the Capital Market Consolidation Act, or the CMCA) will be partially effective on 4 August 2008 and fully implemented on 4 February 2009. Under this legislation, when any financial investment makes an investment recommendation to any non-professional investor, it is required to provide sufficient explanation that the investor understands the financial investment product, the fees involved in investing the structure and characteristics of the financial investment product in terms of investability, the application fees, the terms for early repayment and the matters regarding the termination of or cancellation of contract, and to obtain confirmation of such understanding from the investor by signature, seal, recording or other methods.

Other East Asian Reforms

Vietnam

GDP growth averaged 6.8% per year from 1997 to 2004 even against the background of the Asian financial crisis and a global recession. Since 2001, Vietnamese authorities have reaffirmed their commitment to economic liberalization and international integration and have moved to implement the structural reforms needed to modernize the economy and to produce more competitive, export-driven industries with the economy growing 8.5% in 2007.[2]

Vietnam's membership in the ASEAN Free Trade Area (AFTA) and entry into force of the US-Vietnam Bilateral Trade Agreement in December 2001 have led to even more rapid changes in Vietnam's trade and economic regime, with exports to the US increasing 900% from 2001 to 2007 and, as Vietnam joined the WTO in January 2007 following over a decade long negotiation process, WTO membership has provided Vietnam an anchor to the global market and reinforced the domestic economic reform process.

Korea

Ten years after the Asian financial crisis, South Korea is a net creditor in the world with foreign assets of US$379 billion against foreign debts of US$286 billion and a surplus of US$93 billion in comparison with net foreign debt of US$65 billion just before the outbreak of the 1997 crisis and, in 2006, it had a current account surplus of US$6 billion, capital adequacy ratio above 12% with non-performing loans at a small fraction (less than 1%) of commercial bank assets in end-2006.[3] Thus, the main reason for South Korea's difficulties in 1997 is now believed to be moving beyond its means, borrowing heavily and investing badly. Now a decade later, through hard work, sacrifice and determination, South Korea has slowly recovered from the 1997 aftermath.

By 2008, Korea had built up a formidable foreign exchange reserve, the sixth largest in the world comprising of assets with low risks such as deposits, sovereign bonds, federal agency securities and supernational bonds and, as of September 2008, the total of US$240 billion reserve can be cashed in immediately.[4] The share of household debt relative to the GDP is low compared to that of the US or the UK households, particularly when household assets are taken into account. In 2007, Korea's GDP was KRW901 trillion and the total household debt KRW740 trillion, giving household debt ratio of 82% while corporate debt (KRW940 trillion) relative to the GDP comes to 104% and at end-June 2008, the ratio of household financial liabilities to financial assets stood at 45%, indicating household financial assets exceed liabilities by a factor of 2.22 and thus more than sufficient to offset the liabilities.[5]

Household financial assets and liability growth from 2002 to June 2008, shows that Korean households' financial assets grew at a much faster pace than liabilities (62.6% vs. 57.4%) when compared to those of the US (48.9% vs. 64.6%), the UK (49.3% vs. 64.4%), or Australia (77% vs. 100.8%). It should also be stressed that housing mortgage make up a large portion (60%) of household debt and that an overwhelming majority of the mortgage loans are serviced by stable middle-income households.[6] Corporate debt relative to the GDP has fallen from 131% in 1997 to 104% in 2007 and similarly, Korean companies on the whole have significantly improved their financial soundness over the years by reducing their debt-equity ratio from 424.6% in 1997 to 92.5% (Q1, 2008). In terms of the interest coverage ratio, which is a measure of the debt-servicing ability of companies, improved substantially as well from a factor of 1.2 to 4.1 during roughly the same period.[7]

When domestic banks' overall soundness — for example, their high loan loss provisions against likely future losses — is fully considered together with the overall soundness of household and corporate debt structure, the likelihood of a severe distress stemming from household and corporate loans is low, backed by the consistently low default rates for household bank loans averaging 0.6% as of July 2008 (for mortgage loans, the rate was even lower at 0.4%) and at the end of 2007, the ratio of bank loan provisions to loans classified as substandard or below reached 243.8%.[8]

Afternote

Interestingly, after the 2008 global financial crisis broke out, former United States Federal Reserve Chairman Alan Greenspan admitted that he erred while steering the US economy and now calls for tighter regulation instead of relying on the free market system that he had advocated all these years. Previously, Greenspan had fought off all attempts by the government and politicians to interfere with the market. He regretted fending off controls on financial derivatives which devastated the market and left banks in the US and Europe saddled with billions of dollars of liabilities.

Greenspan now acknowledged the usefulness of regulations in combating fraud and settlement of trade. Philosophically, Greenspan declared that he had made a mistake in assuming the self-interests of organizations like banks and other financial institutions would protect their shareholders and their equity in the firms. He now advocates requirements for banks and securitizers to retain part of the securities they issue. This would motivate companies to ensure assets are properly priced for their risk.

A 27-member group, the Asian Economic Panel, which consisted of well-known US economist Jeffrey Sachs now argue that East Asian macroeconomic policy may be needed to save the current global downturn. East Asia including ASEAN countries, especially Japan, China and Korea can announce joint fiscal expansion tailored to their needs. China would use its funds to construct infrastructure or provide tax cuts while Japan could buy equities on the share markets. They could also use their regulatory powers to cut interest rates and stabilize currencies against a basket of US dollars and Euro. Another possible option is for major East Asian banks (including those in ASEAN) to provide credit swap lines between themselves using the US-Korea swap lines as one example. In general, a coordinated East Asian response, including ASEAN, could produce more sustainable results than through unilateral macroeconomic policies.

CHAPTER 17

The Global Financial Crisis 2008

While calls for reforms went on in East Asia for most of the post-1997 period right up till the late 2000s, warning signs began to emerge on the horizon of a new global economic challenge. Before the outburst of the global financial crisis, which started with a subprime crisis in the US, George Soros, in a visit to Asia (9 January 2006), identified the US current account deficit as one of the key challenges for world economy. He opined that no country now is able or willing to replace the US in driving the global economy through domestic consumption. US consumers continues to be drivers of the global economy. The current account deficit would continue as long as US consumers are happy to spend and the Chinese and other Asians are willing to finance the spending by holding on to US treasury bills and bonds.

On whether the European and Japanese markets would be able to offset any slowdown in the US economy, Mr. Soros thought otherwise. The Europeans are far too interconnected with the US to replace the latter as the world's largest consumer. In fact, a slowdown in the US economy would have the opposite effect with a weaker dollar damaging the competitiveness of European exports and affecting the European economy in the first place.

Japanese growth is optimistic and probably sustainable but is too tied to the Chinese market to make a bigger impact beyond offsetting a small part of US economic decline from deliberate policies to deflate the speculative bubble.

Touching on the topic of American consumption, Soros opined that if the world economy slows down, protectionistic measures might surface. In his view, even collectively, Asian economies would not be able to make up for the slowdown in US consumption. US and consequently world prosperity is funded by a housing financial bubble through speculative real estate boom. To solve this, the Federal Reserve has stepped in to engineer a soft landing.

This would require interest rates to go up so that house prices can be deflated and US consumers made to spend less. Through a gradual adjustment of interest rates, this could then be slowly tuned to a gradual decrease in real estate prices for a soft landing with more frugal expenditure and a slow downsizing of the speculative bubble and imbalances caused by excessive spending and liquidity brought about by inflated real estate prices.

However, he felt this would only have some chance of succeeding and success was not guaranteed. Despite this attempt to engineer a soft landing, Soros felt that the slow tune-down of interests would overshoot because markets react in anticipation. Even after interest rates are decreased to stable level, housing prices and purchases would not recover and would continue to head downwards. Hence is his less-than-optimistic view for the global economy in 2007.

When the slowdown comes, Soros felt that using the Special Drawing Rights (SDRs) within the IMF, a form of global collective to help poor countries draw economic aid in bad times, will come in useful. Such a mechanism already exists but is thwarted by the lack of political will of states to work together. Soros believed that mechanisms such as SDRs would help to mitigate the excesses of market fundamentalism, a flawed belief and assumption that the market would correct itself, which in turn was based on the flawed presumption of perfect knowledge. The missing element here is the lack of sensitivity to collective social needs within the global open market.

Global Financial Crisis Arrives in 2008

Then the global financial crisis happened in 2008. The financial crisis remains on everyone's minds in East Asia, including its political elite. From the micro to the macro political events, the financial crisis has become a hot political issue in the region. For example, in the micro sense, Malaysian candidate for the vice presidency of the ruling party UMNO, Muhyiddin Yassin lists economic recovery as one of the most important agenda for his campaign.

In the Philippines, worries are on how for the first time since the early 1990s, Private Consumption Expenditures (PCE) actually fell between the first and second quarters of 2008. More importantly, there is a pervasive fear that this might result in many overseas Filipinos losing their jobs and remittances back to the Philippines might be severely reduced as a result.

On a much bigger scale, leaders of South Korea, China and Japan held a summit in Fukuoka in December 2008 for discussions on the global financial crisis. Related to this summit, the People's Bank of China announced the establishment of a bilateral currency swap arrangement with the Bank of Korea on 12 December 2008, supporting amounts up to 180 billion yuan or US$39 billion. The arrangement helps to improve short-term liquidity and promote bilateral trade. This comes on the back of South Korea's own bilateral currency swap arrangements with Japan, increasing an existing won-yen arrangement to US$20 billion from US$3 billion that had been in place since May 2005. This upgrading of swap arrangements took place on the same day.

South Korea also already has an agreement that gives it access to US$10 billion from the Bank of Japan in dollars in a crisis while the agreement with China would give them access to 38 trillion yuan at any time for the next three years. A previous agreement with China allows the Korean central bank to get as much as US$4 billion worth of yuan or US dollars during crisis. All three Northeast Asian powerhouses also agreed to initiate regular consultations with each other on currency stability.

This Northeast Asian summit is one positive spin-off from South Korea, China and Japan meeting annually on the sidelines of the Association of Southeast Asian Nations Plus Three (ASEAN+3) summit. Overall, the feeling in East Asia is ambivalent. Some may have a sense of triumphalism. It seems like the West, which had been dispensing harsh advice to East Asian states during the 1997 Asian financial crisis, are now borrowing money from East Asia to tide over the current global financial crisis.

But, East Asia as a whole cannot escape this crisis. US falling demand and the closely-knitted relationship with American institutions will surely worry a large number of Asians. China is much touted as a possible engine of growth in the wake of the US downturn. China's top priority is simply protecting its own economy and tackling unemployment, which is a growing concern as factories are closing down. East Asia may have to work closely with their counterparts in the West to rescue the world from the current crisis. No time to gloat.

Interest rate cuts by five of the world's most influential central banks to cope with the worst financial shakeout seen in 80 years have been carried out. Central banks in England, China, Canada, Sweden and Switzerland, the European Central Bank and the US Federal Reserve eased their key interest rates. IMF's latest assessment is that a global recession or slowdown in world output growth to 3% or less may come in 2009.

CHAPTER 18

Impact and Immediate Response to the Crisis in East Asia

What is the Impact on Major Southeast Asian Economies?

Indonesia

The current financial crisis is expected to hit the Indonesian currency and stock market. In the view of the Indonesian government, a weakening rupiah is manageable as long as it is orderly. Dangers for the Indonesian economy may also come from other countries. Analysts predict that, because of the crisis, China may shift its export destination from the US to countries like Indonesia.

Consequently, some politicians and acting Coordinating Minister for the Economy Sri Mulyani Indrawati are calling for stronger defences against imports of unessential goods and instead promote domestic industries like rattan, wood, tea, coffee, cacao and crude palm oil. Overall, growth would slow to 5.8%, below the government's estimate of 6.2%, precipitated by a decline in exports and imports, as well as in the financial, service and telecommunications sectors.

Indonesia faces the fallout of the global financial crisis when the tight financial conditions can possibly starve its economy of investment capital at a time when it needs funds to augment construction of infrastructure like tolled highways and energy generation. Indonesia's rupiah-denominated debt has also handed investors a loss of 8.2% in 2008, the worst performance of 10 Asian local-currency bond indexes compiled by HSBC Holdings. Pressured by outflow of capital, the rupiah had lost more than a fifth of its value against the US dollar in 2008.

Raising such capital will become harder as interest rates have to be hiked to get foreigners to hold rupiah assets. GDP growth will be limited by the challenges that companies face to get loans for financial expansion and some will have difficulties in paying off overseas debts due to high refinancing costs, resulting in a few high profile corporate failures. Falling global demand may also slow down its exports and lead to unemployment.

Therefore, in October 2008 Indonesia began talks with the World Bank and other lenders to get US$5 billion in standing loans. There are some hopes for optimism in the Indonesian economy. In 1997, Indonesia's short-term loans to foreign reserves ratio stood at 175% but now it stands at 34.5% — indicating no problem with short-term obligations. Bank Indonesia figures for August 2008 also places the capital adequacy ratio of local banks at 16% above the 8% international benchmark set under the Basel Accord. By mid-October 2008, Indonesia's fiscal deficit is equivalent to 1.7% of GDP, releasing some room for prime pumping efforts to cope with the crisis if necessary.

Due to the 1997 lesson, Indonesia reacted fast when its rupiah plunged in late November 2008 in the current bout of the global financial crisis. To manage the crisis, the Indonesian government set up a special Presidential-appointed team of cabinet ministers in the second week of October 2008 including senior bankers and business leaders such as James Riady and Tommy Winanta to come up with policies to counter the economic crisis. Jakarta pledged to respect the free movement of capital in an attempt to shore up investor confidence. Other methods deployed by Jakarta to shore up the declining rupiah include having its state oil regulator insisting on all contractors use local banks to deposit billions of dollars for energy projects to help the currency starting from 20 November 2008.

Indonesia also followed the Malaysian initiative of guaranteeing all foreign and local currency bank deposits which in turn followed the initiative of Hong Kong that led to the positive results of money flowing back into Hong Kong. On 12 October 2008, Indonesia raised the amount of bank deposits it would guarantee. But, some argue that this may not be enough as the government guarantees only a maximum of two billion rupiah per account.

On the trade side, Jakarta's newly enforced health regulations and a late October 2008 Trade Ministry regulation imposing new restrictions on importers of processed food may be non-tariff barriers to protect its domestic industries by enforcing the implementation of the Indonesian National Standard to obstruct imports. This took place against a backdrop of calls for self-reliance and campaigns to buy local products. Indonesia is gripped by nervousness about export-oriented countries dumping their excess production into Indonesia as demand in the developed world slows down. This is backed up by the

Indonesian business lobbyists who are keen to refocus their sales in Indonesia as their traditional export markets dries up.

Politically, this seems to be an expedient thing to do as Indonesian politicians, especially for those that the ruling government is gearing up for the 2009 elections and protecting jobs in Indonesia is seen as extremely important. This is coupled with growing support for shifting away from being an export-oriented economy to developing its own economy based on indigenous resources. For example, especially after China's melamine scandal, the autonomous Food and Drug Monitoring Agency (BPOM), originally a component of the Ministry of Health, has come under fire for not monitoring food products. China's tainted food products thus provided the rationale for Indonesia to limit packaged food imports and to control the way local retailers package foreign-processed food products.

Indonesia has also turned to proactive aggressive measures to tackle the crisis. Indonesia is in crisis mode as its stock market plunged so deeply in October 2008 that it had to close for three days. Indonesia is trying to capitalize on lesser exposure to the global economy and greater reliance on local spending and economy as a way to survive the crisis. It also expects to save US$1.5 billion in 2009 from lower spending on fuel subsidies with the oil price decline and will divert the money for an economic stimulus package. Spending on public infrastructure would also increase to US$9.1 billion (a one-third increase).

Malaysia

Malaysia's politicians, including Tan Sri Second Finance Minister Nor Mohamed Yakcop, continue to insist that positive growth will continue from 2008 to 2009 and that the country is not heading for a recession although the 5.4% growth target for 2009 will have to be recalculated because of the global financial turmoil. But, even the optimistic Second Minister admitted that countries worldwide were going to be affected by the global financial turmoil in some way, depending on the length and extent of the recession in the US and Europe although this was offset by the good news that inflation was no longer a major concern for Malaysia due to the significant drop in the prices of commodities.

Malaysia has other ways to help domestic industries. Malaysia scrapped import taxes on some raw materials (400 products including iron, steel, textiles and chemicals) and also eased up manufacturing license application to cope with global economic downturn with effect from 1 December 2008. By scrapping the import tax, Malaysia is doing exactly the opposite of Indonesia as reduction of import tax will also decrease the government's earnings substantially. Malaysia is also lifting export ban on scrap metal. Malaysia is not modifying its export orientation view in any way.

Malaysia is also injecting an additional RM7 billion (S$3 billion) of public spending into its economy for the construction of affordable housing and publication transportation, to especially prop up its construction industry.

Philippines

The Philippine domestic economy would grow by only 4.4% in 2008 and further slow down to 3.8% in 2009 while the inflation rate was seen to ease to an average of

7% in 2009 from 10.1% in 2008. Annual inflation rate in September 2008 had been lowered to 11.9% from a 17-year peak of 12.5% in August 2008.

Thailand

The advantage enjoyed by East Asian banks is that they have learnt their lessons from the Asian financial crisis of 1997 and have substantial foreign currency reserves and low indebtedness. Thailand for example declared that its government will recapitalize Thai banks if effects from the US financial crisis spill over to the Kingdom. The Thai move came after an explicit warning from the Asian Development Bank (ADB) president Harahiko Kuroda who cautioned Thai finance officials not to be complacent about the spread of the crisis beyond Europe at the annual meeting of the World Bank and the International Monetary Fund in Washington on the second week of October 2008. Kuroda also proceeded to warn Asian banks that they could face trouble even if they had proven to be stronger than the ones in the US and Europe.

Reacting to this warning, the Thai government planned to accelerate budget disbursement to rural areas such as to the SML Fund for villagers to boost grassroots and local economies and stimulate consumption in the process. This is designed to compensate and make up for the expected dip in private investments and export earnings in 2009. The government has also asked for US$500 million to US$1 billion worth of loans from the World Bank and ADB for a mass rapid transit and other logistics projects earmarked for 2009.

Japan

Japan started off with relative insulation from the US subprime crisis and the early stages of the global financial crisis. Initial Japanese media coverage even isolated the US financial woes as the "Lehman Shock" and gave it less coverage than domestic news on typhoon and a tainted rice scandal. According to the IMF, subprime-related losses at Japanese financial companies have totaled just $8 billion, out of global subprime-related losses that some say could total $1 trillion or more.[1] Japanese have an accumulated $14 trillion pile of household savings from trade surpluses and frugal lifestyles to finance its immense $8.1 trillion fiscal deficit and still have enough money left over to be the world's largest creditor nation for the last 17 years.

But Japan's splendid isolation did not last long. The financial crisis with its nucleus in the US saw its big three US automakers plunging into deep financial trouble. Japan's fifth largest automaker, Mazda Motor Co., one-third owned by cash-strapped Ford Motor Co, became an immediate victim as its parent company is putting Mazda up for sale. If Ford is forced to sell off its entire stake and dissolve its joint ventures and projects with Mazda, the Hiroshima-based Mazda will not have enough money to buy back all of the three plants in the US, Thailand and China. Back home, the global financial crisis is hurting Japan's real economy. Demand for Japanese cars had fallen overseas, forcing the Japanese carmaker giant Toyota to slash its forecast earnings in 2008 to less than one-third of the previous year. Japan's carmakers based in the US even had to offer interest-free loans to up its sagging car sales. The continuing credit crisis has also increased the value of the yen over the dollar and other major currencies, eroding the carmakers' profits earned overseas.

Local governments are also feeling the effects. The Toyota city government in Aichi forecasts tax revenue for the next fiscal year will drop by more than 20 billion yen — almost 20% of the 123.4 billion yen forecast for this fiscal year with the impact of cutbacks stemming from this shrinking income trickling down and affecting local residents.[2] In Tahara City of Aichi, which also hosts a Toyota plant, the city has ordered an across-the-board 10% cut on all items in next fiscal year's budget. The city is reviewing plans for projects including road and river maintenance, park improvements and work to improve the earthquake resistance of buildings at primary and middle schools. As a whole Aichi prefecture's tax revenues for next fiscal year will be down by a real 270 billion yen, making up 20% of the prefecture's 1.36 trillion yen.[3]

In other sectors like electronics, an effort to compensate for declining unit prices have seen electronics and computer manufacturers introducing new products, with new models of flat-screen TVs with extra features and specialized digital cameras coming out one after another. In the financial market, as Japanese financial institutions traditionally possess large volumes of shares of various businesses, the strongly bearish state of the stock market has pushed down the mark-to-market value of their equity holdings sharply.

To help the jobless in Japan, the government has offered affordable (monthly rent from 4,000 to 48,000 yen) temporary housing (tenable up to one year) previously reserved for the homeless to the unemployed and the

Finance Ministry alone will put aside 775 units, The Health, Labour and Welfare Ministry will refurbish 31,000 units of rundown housing facilities and rent them out to the unemployed from January 2009 until March 2011 and would provide a discount rate for 23,000 units managed by state-linked housing agency to the unemployed. The Japan Bank for International Cooperation (JBIC) is also doing its part to help Japanese firms operating in the developed world by providing loans available until end March 2010 to exporters as well as big Japanese multi-nationals operating in developing economies.

How is Southeast Asia Coping with the Crisis?

Indonesia's management of the crisis

In the 1997 financial crisis, Indonesia's short-term loans to foreign reserves was at 175% but in this crisis, it is much stronger and stands at 34.5%. Analysts argue that the state can safely finance its short-term loans. The central bank is also downplaying the possibility of a crisis, raising its benchmark interest rate by 25 basis points for six straight months, to 9.5%, signaling to market players that the economy is not going under.

A consistent rise in the BI rate would indicate the central bank was in firm control and guard the economy. BI would monitor the volatility of the rupiah against the dollar, based on global trends. In case of emergencies, some groups have urged the Indonesian government to create a social safety net and provide incentives for exporters and raising the deposit insurance limit from Rp 100 million ($10,325.25) to Rp 250 million.

Malaysia's management of the crisis

Tan Sri Second Finance Minister Nor Mohamed Yakcop pointed out that Malaysia did not experience a banking crisis because it was in a different environment from the US and Europe due to the country's strong banking system with low non-performing loans and a high risk weighted capital ratio. Malaysia has also diversified its economy with exports contributing less than 20% of the growth while domestic consumption and investment have become a major engine of growth and it is producing more goods to China (increased to 9%) and India. Malaysia is banking on China and India to sustain their economic growth.

However, just to be safe, Nor Mohamed said Malaysia needed a social safety net to take care of those who may be vulnerable and that Malaysians need to remain calm and confident about their country's future. According to Nor Mohamed, Malaysia may find opportunities in the crisis, particularly in Islamic banking as funds from the Middle East are losing money in the US and Europe and encouraged to come to Malaysia which is one of the strongest Islamic banking centres in the world. Middle East investors could also invest in infrastructural development projects in Malaysia instead of buying assets in the US and Europe, which have already lost much in terms of value.

Philippines' management of the crisis

Bangko Sentral ng Pilipinas (BSP) Governor Amando Tetangco Jr. noted that moves by the developed countries' central banks have stimulated the BSP in similarly slashing interest rates whenever needed in the future.

BSP Deputy Governor Diwa Guinigundo says the Filipino central bank will hold steady for now. There are fears that the peso might weaken further if they cut rates too soon. The central bank kept its key interest rate and the overnight borrowing rate on hold at 6.0% during a crucial monetary policy setting thus ending a cycle of monetary tightening that had jacked up the rates by a total of 100 basis points. Filipinos are urged to continue to trust in their country's own resilience and economic fundamentals.

CHAPTER 19

Coordinating with the Region and the World

East Asia to the Rescue?

After the US announced its US$700 billion bailout package for Wall Street, Japanese Prime Minister Taro Aso went on public record on 16 October 2008 to say that the US bailout was insufficient and contributed to plunges in the stock market (Japan's key stock index fell 10% on the same day on 16 October 2008). It therefore dawned upon East Asian governments that their resources might be needed for the rescue, especially since Japan has more than US$950 billion in foreign exchange reserves next to China's US$1.9 trillion. In 1997, during the last Asian financial crisis, an event which somewhat affected her image as the economic leader in the region, Japan actually pledged a US$80 billion fund to help Southeast Asian economics.

Governments to the Rescue

Asia's wealthiest governments are moving fast to guarantee bank deposits for their citizens. Hong Kong and Australia were amongst the first to do so. Hong Kong was especially unnerved by depositors responding to unfounded rumors of financial foundations of banks (e.g. Bank of East Asia) by withdrawing their deposits in droves. This was followed by New Zealand, which guaranteed all retail bank deposits for two years. Japan, Asia's economic superpower, is also considering a blanket guarantee for all bank deposits after already instituting an initiative to protect savings of up to 10 million yen (approximately $100,000).

Other Southeast Asian economies have their own protective measures. Indonesia, which is Southeast Asia's largest economy, increased the limit on deposit protection to the level which savings are guaranteed by twenty times to two billion rupiah (206,000 dollars). In the Philippines, deposit insurance covers savings of up to 250,000 pesos (5300 dollars), protecting 95% of accounts. Such decisions were made from taking their cues from European countries which institute similar policies. Other Southeast Asian countries have no need for such measures. In Vietnam, less than 6% of the population has a bank account, with families traditionally putting their wealth in gold and property. Other than guarantees, East Asian countries earlier this year proposed an $80 billion currency swap agreement, expanding a much more modest agreement that was set up in the wake of the 1997/98 Asian financial crisis to protect any country facing a balance of payments crisis.

New solutions are needed because Americans cannot spend as they do before and therefore household consumption can be expected to go down sharply. The write downs in US household wealth from the reversals in housing and equities will probably reach US$15 trillion (S$22 trillion) and the resulting steep decline in private consumption and investment could reach one-tenth of that amount.[1]

Macroeconomic policies are now needed to arrest a global meltdown. One of the strategies being floated around to change and reform Asian policy regimes has been calls to abandon the old strategy of export-oriented growth and high domestic savings. They have suggested dependence on alternative strategies like greater reliance on domestic demand and high consumption rather than excess savings.

Malaysia which had adopted unusual macroeconomic fiscal policies to combat the 1997 Asian financial crisis is again one of the earliest East Asian states to institute decisive coping strategies this round. Najib Razak, Malaysia's incoming Prime Minister scheduled to take office in March 2009, carefully unfurled his strategy to deal with the global economic crisis. The difficulties that he would face in tackling the crisis was indicated early by the defiance posed by the opposition politicians under the leadership of Anwar Ibrahim who staged a parliamentary walkout to protest their claims that they were not allowed to properly debate the 2009 budget.

Najib cut the 2009 growth forecast to 3.5% from 5.4% and said the budget deficit would be 4.8% of GDP, up from the previous projected 3.6%. To combat the crisis, Najib plans to transfer almost $2 billion to be saved from fuel subsidies into infrastructure construction projects and to reduce pension fund contributions from 11% to 8%. This will help to place more money in the hands of Malaysians.

Najib also worked fast to shore up foreign investor confidence by instituting attractive measures to allow foreign investors to own up to 70% of firms in the service sector from 2015. Najib's fast and decisive policies is designed to make maximum impact to avoid a technical recession and help to restore trust amongst Malaysians towards the Barisan Nasional coalition that has governed Malaysia for 51 years but for the first time, lost its two-thirds majority power in the 2008 election, to change the constitution.

Boosting Domestic Consumption

Another idea floated around East Asia is boosting domestic consumption. All over East Asia, governments are encouraging spending amongst their populations. Vietnam is one of the first to put this into practice. Given the devastating effect of the financial crisis in the US, consumer demand for imported goods has slowed down considerably. The EU, which also faces a credit crunch, also has lower demands for Vietnamese apparels and textiles. This has prompted Vietnamese garment makers to focus more on their home market since overseas exports, their engine of growth, may be reduced considerably. The slowdown in demand is particularly worrisome for Vietnam as it is the world's ninth largest exporter of textiles.

In order to focus on domestic demand, new strategies need to be planned since Vietnamese home industries would have to compete with foreign imports into the country. Apparels accounted for 5% of the country's $45 billion retail market in 2008. Consumers in the 20 to 45 age group in Ho Chi Minh City spend 18.5% of their income on clothes. Another strategy is to go up-market and generate higher value-added products by producing branded and better quality clothes to compete with foreign imports. Vietnamese companies like TCM, Tay Do, Legamex, F-House, An Phuoc, Viettien, Foci, and Ninomaxx are likely to lead this charge.

Vietnam is not the only country implementing such measures to boost domestic consumption. One possible prescription for China to recalibrate its economic model and become an engine of growth is to stoke domestic investment with heavy government spending and promote policies to increase consumer spending in a nation famous for high savings rates.

Some countries such as Thailand, have even suggested a hybrid model of continuing with a export-oriented economy while building up domestic markets. Until recently, China was tightening up its monetary and fiscal policies to combat inflation but now it must change course to augment its domestic consumption demand and take the burden of a coordinated expansion throughout the East Asian region.

Japan and South Korea would be involved in this venture. Some possible options for China include increasing infrastructure spending and building public housing. In Japan, infrastructure building has been a familiar solution while it can dispense more loans to developing countries in Africa and other parts of Asia for capacity-building and infrastructure construction by Japanese companies. A trilateral effort amongst the three most powerful and economically strong countries in East Asia is needed. South Korea, China and Japan can cooperate with regional central banks in the area of expansionary policies backed by government-to-government loans.

Prime-pumping is seen as a possible panacea by some economists and policy-makers. Analysts in Nomura for example has urged the government to boost government spending on research and development (e.g. in fossil fuel alternatives), medical healthcare and education on top of the classic infrastructure building to boost domestic consumption.

Japanese Prime Minister Taro Aso unveiled a 26.9 trillion yen (US$401.6 billion) package on 30 October 2008 to jump-start Asia's largest economy, which includes tax cuts mainly targeted at households and small businesses. This is the second package after Yasuo Fukuda's first stimulus initiatives instituted in late August 2008 aimed at easing the hardship caused by rising commodity prices. Japan is spending 5 trillion yen or 2% of its GDP in direct cash payouts to families, tax breaks on mortgages, bank rescue schemes in public fund injections and tax relief for small firms. A 27-trillion yen stimulus package initiated on 30 October 2008 by the Aso administration sees that each Japanese get 12,000 yen (S$200) and children under 18 and elderly over 65 getting an extra 8,000 yen each.

Out of this stimulus package, two trillion yen will be dispensed to Japanese households in one lump sum payment by March 2009. A family of four can receive an estimated 60,000 yen which families can choose to spend and if this happens, it is a de facto stimulus package. Other economic goodies include consumers having larger tax deductions on their home mortgages and an extension of current tax reductions on capital gains and dividends and, to boost the use of highways outside the metropolitan urban areas, traffic tolls will be reduced to a maximum of 1,000 yen for car owners on vacation.

2.3 trillion yen is spent to cover the increase in the portion of the basic pension program covered by the central government from one-third of the total to one-half and another one trillion yen was included in the budget draft as a reserve fund to deal with future economic emergencies. The goodies are not just restricted to individual consumers, they extend to the corporate sector where increased loan guarantees for small and medium sized firms is the largest component of the stimulus package, with the goal of easing the credit crunch that small companies may experience as banks reduce lending.

China has also moved to prevent a US-like property meltdown. Property prices has been falling from the second quarter of 2008 with growth reduced to 5.3% compared to August 2008 and Shenzhen's property prices was down 40% from the peak a year before, prompting the Chinese local governments to lower transaction levies, direct subsidies and tax incentives and in places like Shanghai, the maximum sum first time home buyers can loan from the government was doubled to 200,000 Chinese yuan.[2]

China is also spending four trillion yuan or 16% of its GDP on large-scale infrastructure projects such as railways, roads and airports. One trillion of which will be used to rebuild areas damaged by the May 2008 Sichuan earthquake. Hong Kong is spending HK\$19.3 billion or 1.2% of its GDP in 66 small scale projects to create over 12,000 jobs and the early initiation of the construction of a mega bridge to link Hong Kong, Zhuhai and Macau to 2009 instead of 2010.

Across the Straits, Taiwan is giving its 23 million citizens NT\$3,600 shopping vouchers each during the traditional Chinese New Year celebrations to augment spending amongst its population. They are valid until September 2009. Sensing an opportunity for better relations, China pledged to provide S$27 billion or 130 billion yuan in financing through three Chinese banks for Taiwanese small and medium sized enterprises (SMEs) based in the mainland on 21 December 2008 at the fourth annual cross-straits economic forum in Shanghai attended by 400 scholars and officials from both sides of the Straits.

These SMEs would be accorded the same tax and loan policies as other local Chinese businesses in China. These are acknowledgement of Taiwan's contributions to the mainland with investments of US$64.9 billion in China in 2007 according to Taiwanese estimates. Thus, it is China's turn to cushion the pain from the financial crisis for some of these companies that are facing challenges. In exchange, both China and Taiwan agreed to allow companies to participate in public infrastructure projects in each other locations.

In Southeast Asia, Thailand is one of the first countries to declare its intentions to intervene in the economy as the global financial crisis worsens. Finance Minister Suchart Thadathamrongvech said that the government will recapitalize its banks if the effects from the US financial crisis spill over to Thailand. Even though Asian banks are stronger in capitalization, Minister Suchart revealed that he was personally warned by the Asian Development Bank (ADB) president Harahiko Kuroda to be vigilant in monitoring the situation if the crisis spreads beyond Europe.[3]

The Thai government will also speed up budget allocations to rural areas such as the SML fund for villagers as a means of boosting the grassroots local economies to stimulate consumption to combat the slowdown in private investments and export revenue in 2009. The Thai government has also requested for US$500 million to US$1 billion loans from the World Bank and ADB for mass transportation and logistics projects.[4]

Malaysia is expending RM7 billion or 1.1% of its GDP with RM5 billion for construction and upgrading of infrastructure such as schools, high-speed broadband, hospitals, roads, low cost housing and government buildings. RM600 million is also allocated for worker training programmes. Malaysia has set up a Corporate Debt Restructing Committee to bring creditors and debtors together for coordination to bring about stability and similar bodies were initiated in Indonesia as well as South Korea in Northeast Asia. Thus, there is an active process of learning from each other.

Looking Beyond the Crisis

Some East Asian governments are already doing strategic thinking to look at the post-crisis period. They argue that, having been conservative and consistent in the delivery of economic performance, East Asian governments need to utilize the current period of economic crisis to augment themselves and look for new opportunities. The strategy, it seems, is not to be complacent and mock the perceived Western-inspired crisis or switch completely to caution and pessimism that can restrict future economic growth. The trick is also to be vigilant for sudden downturns while keeping an eye out for good investments.

China, for example, is quietly spending and shoring up its financial assets in the UK stock markets. Since January 2008, the British blue chip index, the FTSE100, has fallen nearly 19% by the first week of September 2008. But the People's Bank of China, the PRC's central bank's agency the State Administration of Foreign Exchange (SAFE), started to accumulate approximately US$22.7 billion worth of shares in British industries.

With four global offices in New York, London, Hong Kong and Singapore, SAFE is now ranked amongst the top 25 investors in the London stock market. This sum that is spent in the UK represents only a small portion of China's US$1.7 trillion of foreign exchange holdings, each month this sum of money increases by approximately US$80 billion.[5] SAFE is authorized to accumulate stakes of up to 1% in a long list of FTSE100 and some FTSE250 companies; SAFE as a whole will move 5% of its portfolio into shares (US$85 billion) and transform it into one of the largest sovereign wealth funds in the world but making up only one month's reserve accumulation in China.[6]

The IMF estimates that Sovereign Wealth Funds (SWFs) in Asia and the Middle East as well as other regions collectively hold total assets of between US$1.9 to US$2.8 trillion. Southeast Asian countries are also starting new SWFs. Mooted by Malaysian King Sultan Mizan Zainal Abidin, Malaysia is introducing greater transparency into the use of its oil royalties by setting up a SWF with a seed capital of RM10 billion (S$4.2 billion) to manage Terengganu's petroleum revenues through a committee made up by professionals that are not politically-motivated. This would also avoid the mismanagement of the past. The King himself would head a board of advisors but cannot intervene with veto powers on the management of the fund. Some viewed the use of oil revenue to construct theme parks and events such as the Monsoon Cup international sailing competition as white elephants and non-productive prestige events.

But SWFs also run into risks from unpredictable instability in the market. Their multibillion injections into Western entities at good bargain prices see their value sharply reduced by deteriorating market conditions. Often these are not due to the fault of the SWFs and are beyond their control. Thus, some SWFs are asking for protection.

Emanating from the last US-China Strategic Economic Dialogue for the Bush Administration on 6 December 2008, and strained by the increasing depressive effects of the crisis, the US has instituted a rapid approval process of Chinese financial institutions that want to invest in the US. In return, China has called on the US to ensure the safety of Chinese assets and investments in the US. This was because, up till the first week of December 2008, the US$200 billion SWF, China Investment Corp (CIC) has lost US$6 billion on stake purchases in Morgan Stanley and Blackstone Group. The exact mechanism in which the US can help to safeguard Chinese assets in the US will be something that both countries will have to work out under the Obama Administration.

CHAPTER 20

ASEAN Economic Regionalism: A Regional Financial Architecture in the Making?

Prior to the Asian financial crisis in 1997, rapid and dynamic economic growth in Southeast Asia was facilitated through market-driven forces. Various regional economic cooperation initiatives and schemes were introduced, including an agreement on the ASEAN Free Trade Area (AFTA) in 1992, which came into full operation by end of 2003. However, the net impact of ASEAN-initiated regional cooperation was negligible because ASEAN economies were basically competing on the same product range and their main export markets were to non-ASEAN members, i.e. the United States, European Union and other developed economies.

It is often said that ASEAN as a regional organization is more effective in 'pooling resources' rather than in 'sharing market'. As a result of this structural economic and political reality, it is not the regional governments that have been driving regional economic integration but rather the globalization process and transnational corporations that are driving the process.

The economic collapse of many Southeast Asian economies after the Asian financial crisis paved the way for the establishment of ASEAN+3 (China, Japan and South Korea) framework or regional economic cooperation. Underlying this fundamental change in regional approach for economic integration are the emerging elements of the rise of China and India, weakening of multilateral trading system and structural imbalances in ASEAN economies weakened by the financial and economic crisis in 1997. It seems without a closer and strengthened economic integration with Northeast Asian economies, ASEAN economies would experience prolonged structural disequilibrium to restore their economic dynamism. Due to the absence of a framework of cooperation in Northeast Asia, specifically because of the bilateral relations between China and Japan, ASEAN has become the default 'hub' of East Asia economic integration. Regional economic integration in de facto sense has been accelerating.

ASEAN regional cooperation on trade and investment cannot be seen in isolation from the group's broader thrust on economic integration. The latter gained momentum with the birth of AFTA in 1992, and accelerated after the 1997 Asian financial crisis. The late 1990s saw a surge in interest in regionalism in ASEAN and East Asia. The movement towards an ASEAN Economic Community (AEC), part of the ASEAN Vision 2020, was also started based on existing initiatives such as the AFTA, ASEAN Framework Agreement on Services (AFAS) and ASEAN Investment Area (AIA). There have also been economic cooperation arrangements on a sub-regional level such as in Growth Triangles (GT).

The launching of the Initiative for ASEAN Integration (IAI) Work plan is the response of ASEAN in assisting its less fortunate members bridge the development gap among the older and newer members. Concerned about the well-being of their fellow members, ASEAN-6 countries have committed to make significant contributions to uplift the standards of living of the CLMV countries in line with the concept of self help. The IAI Work Plan for CLMV focuses on the priority areas of Infrastructure Development (Transport and Energy), Human Resource Development (Public Sector Capacity Building, Labour & Employment, and Higher Education), Information and Communications Technology, and Promoting Regional Economic Integration (Trade in Goods and Services, Customs, Standards and Investments) in the CLMV countries.

In ASEAN's attempts at regional integration, some problems remain. Access to finance, in particular term lending, is a major problem for the industry as the banking sector in the Lao PDR is in a weak position to serve the manufacturing sector; four major institutions holding two-thirds of the banking assets and almost 80% of total deposits are insolvent.[1]

Difficulties in enforcement of the Bankruptcy Law and the Secured Transaction Law through the court system as well as the lack of a system for centralized registration of mortgages hamper banks' willingness to provide credits to the industry, even when collateral is available. An overall financial sector reform programme is ongoing and should yield some positive results over time. As part of this programme, the Government may also study the viability of new instruments such as a credit guarantee scheme, an export credit guarantee scheme, leasing, venture capital funds etc.

Institutions are foundational to successful free market systems. As the CLMV countries transit from a centrally-planned to a market economy, there needs to be a shift in the legal and regulatory frameworks, which are still weak in the CLMV countries. The scope of the IAI should be broadened to include exchange at a leadership level, for economically more advanced countries to lend their expertise in policy-making. But the exchange should not be one-way, there needs to be a dialogue so that reforms suit the CLMV countries' individual unique circumstance. This would also be a step towards political integration. Further, trade liberalization and economic integration would achieve more if they are supported by reforms in the inefficient state-owned enterprises (SOE) sector and banking system.

Subregional Strategies to Cope with Financial Crisis

Besides ASEAN-wide initiatives, there are also subregional strategies in East Asia to fight the crisis. As the East Asian region prepares the details for a mooted US$80 billion fund to cope with the global financial crisis, subregional cooperation is being revved up as well. Leaders from the Mekong subregion (Thailand, Cambodia, Laos, Myanmar and Vietnam) gathered in Vietnam on 7 November 2008 for the Ayeyawady–Chao Phraya–Mekong Economic Cooperation Strategy (ACMECS) Forum to formulate joint approaches in coping with the financial crisis in anticipation of a slowdown in foreign developmental aid and FDIs. The poorest countries in the subregion are extremely worried.

The convener of the Forum, Vietnam's PM Nguyen Tan Dung focused on augmenting transport, trade and investment amongst the Mekong states as one possible avenue to cope with the crisis. Then Thailand's Prime Minister Somchai Wongsawat pointed out the region has been affected by volatility oil and food prices and wants to put the agenda of rice price stabilization on the table. Cambodia's Hun Sen focused on the need for an innovative mechanism for project financing.

Another way is to enhance closer mutual transport (highways and bridges) and commercial links with the economic power of neighbour China. In the spirit of sub-regional self-help, Thailand volunteered to finance a third Mekong river bridge to Laos between the northeastern city of Nakorn Phanom and Kam Muan. All these are done in the hope that the subregion can integrate faster for augmenting trade and investment and lessen the hassles of border inspection and customs rules.

The ACMECS group is targeting seven areas in economic development: telecommunication, tourism, trade and investment, agriculture, industry and energy, human resource development and public health development. In the area of tourism, a declaration to work towards the "Five Nations, One Destination" tourism scheme is seen as a test case of political wills.

Actors in East and South Asia Outside ASEAN

How are they plugging into ASEAN's regionalism initiatives?

In late August 2008, ASEAN reaped a triple play by finalizing deals with India, China, Australia and New Zealand. This includes a comprehensive deal with goods, services and investments with Australia and New Zealand. The

Bush administration also welcomed the decisions of Peru and Australia to join the US, Singapore, Chile, New Zealand and Brunei in negotiating a regional free trade pact that has grown out of the APEC organization.

Meanwhile, China is seen as the shining star of East Asia with her tourism potential as well as demand for raw materials stimulating Southeast Asian economies. In terms of economic cooperation between ASEAN and China, Southeast Asia realized that there are three roles that China can play. First, China can increase her consumption of goods produced by neighbouring countries, including ASEAN, sharing its economic fruits with others in the region. Secondly, China can be a stabilizer of regional currencies by holding fast to its renminbi peg and hence lessening the risk of a financial crisis in the region sparked off by currency fluctuations. Thirdly, ASEAN–China Free Trade Agreement (ACFTA) can help to cushion the fall-out in the region from China's growing economy if implemented by allowing ASEAN countries to have an expected head-start in exporting goods to China.

FTA with India — finance on the agenda

ASEAN is also reaching out to India. In India's negotiations of an FTA with ASEAN, it considers the following service sectors to be its priority in the FTA negotiations with India: finance, education, health, IT & telecommunication, transport (including infrastructure), movement of professionals and other business services. India hopes to fill in the "emerging increasingly skill-scarce [gap] in a relative cost effective sense" with its professionals and "then provide opportunities for India to access third country markets through partnering with an established ASEAN service firm in the targeted host country."[2]

They are aware of ASEAN's competitiveness in the service sector: "ASEAN service firms (especially those from ASEAN5) have both exported a range of services to OECD countries and also invested in a range of sectors like: education, healthcare, professionals and specialists, business support services, construction and engineering (including architecture and surveying), infrastructure development and real estate services, commerce (wholesale and retail trade), transport and tourism, financial services (including pension fund management) and telecommunication services."[3]

Thus, the strategy from India's angle is to leverage on the ASEAN–India FTA to enable Indian service providers to partner with established ASEAN service firms to service third country markets. Priority in the negotiations is not placed on opening up India's services market for ASEAN entries. Due to this strategy, the Indians will be robust in dealing with ASEAN on the services sector.

The FTA negotiations strategy in dealing with ASEAN recommended by the Indian Council for Research on International Economic Relations (ICRIER) is perhaps reflective of this robustness. Amongst other issues during negotiations, the ICRIER recommends that India focus on financial services: banking, insurance, securities and broking, financial advisory, consumer finance, etc.

China's and India's economic rise has driven home the realization for ASEAN countries that it would be critical for them to restructure and integrate their economies in order to sustain their competitiveness. ASEAN political leaders accept this, and envisage that the creation of an economically integrated ASEAN with a combined population of 500 million would strengthen competitiveness, not least by increasing its attractiveness as a host region for foreign investors.

CHAPTER 21

Forming an Economic Community

ASEAN Economic Community

It was in this spirit that ASEAN leaders agreed to explore the possibility of creating an ASEAN Economic Community (AEC) by the year 2020. The AEC is to provide the necessary framework to enhance economic integration within ASEAN and will also facilitate in realizing the economic component of the ASEAN Vision 2020 to create a stronger and more prosperous ASEAN.

With AEC as the ultimate goal, ASEAN started a process of inter-linkages through various relatively less ambitious schemes first. ASEAN has done much to continue with policies that emphasize economic development and openness, despite the 1997 crisis and the rising doubts about globalization. Several member states experienced a sharp 'V'-shaped recovery, prior to the global downturn in 2000. Bold measures and an acceleration of the AFTA commitments were declared. Processes for the exchange of financial information, surveillance and a framework for bilateral currency swaps have been agreed for greater financial predictability and stability among ASEAN member states and others in Asia.

Arrangements arising out of economic cooperation between ASEAN and Northeast Asia, a collaboration known as the East Asian Community or ASEAN+3, also contribute to the realization of AEC. Most notably, financial integration through the Chiang Mai Initiative (CMI) and Asian Bonds Markets Initiative is instrumental in facilitating trade and investment.

Regional Currency

Cooperation in finance began with the Chiang Mai Initiative of bilateral currency swap arrangements between a number of ASEAN and the Plus Three countries and cooperation in finance was expected to be the main driver towards East Asia economic integration. But, this swap arrangement has yet to be multilateralized as its amount is far from sufficient and the group also needs to produce a credible surveillance process before the arrangement can be strengthened. Progress has not been as rapid as expected initially.

It is still too early to tell if this currency swap will eventually grow to a full-blown regional currency. A senior official of the Asian Development Bank (ADB), Mr. Masahiro Kawai, the head of ADB's regional integration office, has warned that Asian governments should not take the continued stability of the US dollar for granted.[1] Instead, they should appreciate their currencies through joint efforts. The governments in East Asia have the largest foreign reserves in the world but most of these funds are invested overseas, particularly to the US. China has reportedly overtaken Japan to become the world's largest holder of foreign exchange reserves, with $853.7 billions as of February.

This call comes in the midst of the run-up of a US Treasury publication to Congress on whether any country in the world is unfairly manipulating its currency to gain unfair advantages against US companies. The US Treasury is expected to publish its report on 15 April 2008, just days before Chinese President Hu Jintao visits Bush. The ADB also said on 27 March 2008 that it would be working towards the creation of an Asian Currency Unit (ACU), which would be an index of currencies, similar to the European Currency Unit (ECU).[2] The ECU was the forerunner of the Euro. ADB is still examining which currencies to include in the ACU and the relative weights. The creation of the ACU is seen as part of the ongoing efforts to promote monetary and financial cooperation in East Asia after the Asian Financial Crisis in 1997–1998.

It is likely the ACU could be a useful denominator for bond issues and facilitate the development of an Asian multi-currency bond market. It would also deepen capital markets, a move which would reduce external monetary shocks. This would also help the region to use some of their financial reserves for investments (particularly infrastructural projects) at home as pointed out earlier by ADB's Vice President Liqun Jin at the Mekong Development Forum held on 8 March. However, ADB President, Haruhiko Kuroda has emphasized, in an earlier interview, that any single Asian Currency like that of the Euro is likely to be decades away. He said that such a single currency is a "very remote possibility." He explained that, "Before we can realistically envisage any single currency, we have to have a single market as the European experience shows."

There are also many issues still unresolved and may become politicized. While the ACU is likely to be based on ASEAN+3 countries, it is uncertain as to whether the Indian rupee would also be included. And already there are potential heated argument over whether the Taiwanese dollar should be included. Another potentially difficult issue is how the weights of the various currencies should be calculated — whether by gross domestic product, trade flows or financial transactions or a combination of the various elements.

Regional bond market

Some have argued for a roadmap for the creation of an ASEAN regional bond market (ARBM), that is, an integrated system within which cross-issuance of fixed income securities would be possible, consistent with the Hanoi Plan of Action. This will help the AEC process by strengthening ASEAN financial development in general by reducing the need for extra-regional intermediation; increasing the participation in the regional market on both the demand and supply sides of the market; including higher participation by international players; creating greater diversity in the financial system with more efficient portfolio diversification/debt management for the private sector, quasi-governmental institutions, and governments; reducing to a minimum the currency and maturity mismatches.

The ASEAN+3 Asian Bond Markets Initiative (ABMI) scheme, which finance ministers agreed to promote in 2003, aims to develop efficient and liquid bond markets in Asia, so that Asian savings can be better utilized for Asian investments. Projects under the ABMI generally fall into two areas: 1) facilitating market access through increasing the range of issuers and types of bonds, and

2) improving market infrastructure to strengthen bond markets.

Establishing a Crisis Fund

The news first broke from Manila on 15 October 2008 that Filipino President Gloria Macapagal-Arroyo declared that Southeast Asian nations, backed by Japan, China and South Korea, have agreed to set up a multi-billion dollar fund to buy toxic debt and help to recapitalize the region's banks and private companies. She also claimed that the World Bank has committed to initially provide $10 billion to the fund.

President Arroyo claimed that the plans were drawn up at the World Bank/IMF meetings in Washington in the week preceding 15 October 2008. President Arroyo also added her own interpretation of the fund. She continued elaborating the role of World Bank and the IMF, with the help of ASEAN finance ministers and central bank governors, would draft the implementing mechanism for disbursing funds and, in her view, hopefully with minimal conditions attached.

According to President Arroyo's statement, the World Bank and the IMF are working closely with ASEAN finance ministers and central bank governors to construct the mechanism for distributing the funds and the conditions attached to the funds. Many in East Asia hope that the conditions will not be onerous.

Arroyo's announcement was followed by her Trade Secretary's. Arroyo's Trade Secretary Peter Favilla said on 16 October 2008 to offer some clarification that the World Bank was working on a facility to provide liquidity to troubled countries around the world, although it had earlier discussed contributing $10 billion to an ASEAN fund. He threw further confusion into the issue when he noted that the World Bank was actually looking at providing the funds on a Bank-wide global facility and that it appeared the initiative is not solely for ASEAN. In his view, the World Bank is now shifting the discussions from a regional facility to a bilateral one. Then, on 17 November, Philippine Economic Planning Secretary Ralph Recto said it was the IMF, and not the World Bank, which floated the possibility of a $10 billion credit facility during the IMF/World Bank annual meeting in Washington.

But, the Arroyo announcement and her Trade Secretary's comments were greeted with puzzlement, caution and confusion from different quarters. The Asian Development Bank (ADB) said it was too early to talk of contributions to the facility because the region remains strong. Analysts said there was no immediate need to recapitalize banks or companies in Asia as few were exposed to the crisis in the West. On 17 October 2008, a World Bank official said the bank has no plans to contribute to the fund, while the ADB said it was too early to talk of contributions because the region was economically sound and in no imminent danger from global turmoil.

It was also unclear why Arroyo made the announcement, rather than Thailand, the current chairman of ASEAN although there was speculation fueled by a Thai official who said it could be because of political problems in the country. Analysts offered possible explanations for the Arroyo announcement, stating she could have been misinformed, or had jumped the gun on what was basically a scenario exercise.

Some also pointed to the premature timing of Arroyo's announcement, which may have taken hints from South Korea's suggestion of a new international organization mandated to address cross-border economic issues such as the current financial crisis.

At the outset of this announcement, it was unclear if this initiative is different from the agreements made by East Asian countries earlier in 2008 which proposed an $80 billion currency swap agreement, expanding a much more modest agreement that was set up in the wake of the 1997–1998 Asian financial crisis to protect any country facing a balance of payments crisis. Some see this expansion of reserve pooling scheme as a step closer to creating a full-scale Asian monetary fund, which has gained support in Asia as the financial turmoil dampens growth. That scheme which Arroyo coined as Chiang Mai 2 will replace the existing arrangement of mainly bilateral currency swaps formed after the 1997–1998 Asian financial crisis, known as the Chiang Mai Initiative.

Though Arroyo may have been premature in announcing a regional rescue fund, discussions have been taking place across Asia over finding common approaches to a financial storm that originated in First World financial centers but which is buffeting emerging economies.

The annual Asia-Europe summit (October 24–25) in Beijing became the first real opportunity to clear Arroyo's remarks once and for all. 13 East and Southeast Asian nations agreed on 24 October 2008 Friday to an $80 billion pool of central bank swap lines. It became the first major coordinated regional action since the full force of the financial turmoil erupted last month.

The Korean government added more details to the initiative. The fund is scheduled to be established by the end the first half of 2009 and establish an independent regional financial market surveillance organization.

In accordance with international media report, in May 2008 East Asian nations reached a preliminary agreement to create a foreign exchange reserve pool of $80 billion. In addition, the initial agreement called for South Korea, Japan and China to provide 80% or $64 billion, with ASEAN members providing the remaining $16 billion. After the summit, President Arroyo on 26 October 2008 added further comments that she wanted a December summit of Asian powers to ease conditions on a regional financial support arrangement and to bring forward its launch to counter global economic woes. Arroyo also said she wanted leaders to ease conditions on the use of the pool, 80% of which is tied to stringent conditions of the IMF. She wanted a less cumbersome multilateralized system that can facilitate a quicker dispersing of funds to be implemented sooner, rather than later. In her view, anything less than that may be too difficult for an economy that is in trouble to access on time. She also proposed that the scheme's launch be brought forward to December 2008, when ASEAN member states will hold a summit with China, Japan and South Korea.

In the final analysis, one interpretation of the so-called ASEAN+3/Chiang Mai initiatives is that, strictly speaking the Chiang Mai initiative is meant for currency swap in case any currency or a group of currencies of the ASEAN+3 countries is under severe pressure (as was the case in 1997). In a broader context, the Chiang Mai initiative for financial and monetary cooperation can be interpreted to be used to stabilize financial instability in the region. There is no specific mention for bailing out banks. It is very much at the discretion of ASEAN+3 policy-makers (Ministries of Finance and Central Banks) what financial and monetary policies are needed to stabilize financial crisis.

Arroyo's views have not been officially endorsed by ASEAN and remain Philippines' proposed points at the moment. Anticipating opposition, the Filipino media noted that Ms Arroyo's proposal could easily be resisted by other members of ASEAN+3 that are wary of putting their funds at greater risk but she appeared eager to lobby China as a potential backer.

What is clear, however, is that East Asian nations agreed at the summit to create an $80 billion joint fund by June 2009 (end of first half) to manage the economic downturn. Initial details indicate that the Northeast Asian powerhouses South Korea, Japan and China would provide 80% or $64 billion while ASEAN members provide the remaining $16 billion. They also agreed to establish an independent regional financial market surveillance organization.

This crisis fund is as historical as it is significant. The deal between South Korea, China, Japan and the ten members of ASEAN is the first major coordinated regional East Asian action. It also moves one step forward from the past as this ASEAN+3 fund would supersede the Chiang Mai Initiative (*circa* year 2000) in the wake of the 1997–1998 East Asian financial crisis to ease mainly bilateral currency swaps. It also represents one major step forward from the 2006 talks on transforming the Chiang Mai Initiative into a more powerful and multilateral reserve pooling mechanism.

But practical limitations of such crisis fund are apparent immediately. In fact, right after the solidarity was shown, a massive sell-off came as Asian leaders meeting in Beijing agreed to set up an $80 billion fund to fight the global economic crisis. Japanese shares fell sharply after a profit warning from technology giant Sony. In addition, some expect disagreements between South Korea, China and Japan on cost-sharing and the way the fund would be managed to be future obstacles. Nevertheless, the action of setting up the fund is symbolic of collective action by East Asians to exert long-term ownership of their future regional financial destiny in their own hands.

Although her earlier statement about a crisis fund set up by the World Bank was somewhat premature and denied by the world organization, thirteen East and Southeast Asian nations have agreed in Beijing during an ASEAN Plus three meeting to an $80 billion crisis fund. Now, President Arroyo wants more haste and flexibility in easing conditions on a regional financial support arrangement to combat global economic woes. Arroyo is still unhappy about the fact that 80% of which is tied to stringent conditions of the IMF, describing it as cumbersome.

The key word in her own proposal for the crisis fund is quick-dispersing of funds to allow East Asian nations in trouble to access funds on time. Arroyo also wants the details to be ironed out during the ASEAN member states' summit with China, Japan and South Korea in December 2008. Such proposals are said to have been met by fierce opposition from fellow ASEAN member countries but Arroyo is persistent on lobbying China to back her plan.

Some see this ASEAN+3 reserve pooling initiative as an early step towards creating an Asian monetary fund. Optimistic about its future, Arroyo nicknames the $80 billion crisis fund as Chiang Mai 2. Besides this crisis fund, Arroyo is also busy rallying China and other Asian powers attending the G20 summit in Washington to represent the worries of developing countries and their poor in this current bout of financial crisis. Arroyo hopes that the crisis would present an opportunity for developing countries, including those in the oil-rich Middle East to become more important investors in Asia.

Other than the proposed ASEAN+3 Fund, in a call for ASEAN solidarity, on 10 November 2008, the Philippines and Thailand agreed that on unity within ASEAN in facing the global financial crisis. Thailand is the chairman of ASEAN and hosts the Asian summit in mid-December 2008 in Chang Mai. The Philippines received former Thai PM Somchai with red-carpet treatment and military honors when he arrived at the Filipino Malacañang palace. Both countries agreed that the poor in Southeast Asia and their long-term needs should be given priority in any proposed co-ordinated solutions and that there is a need for greater confidence.

They also instituted this united front ahead of the G20 in Washington. Stressing on intra-ASEAN trade, President Arroyo noted that Thai companies such as Siam Cement and Dusit Hotel are investors in the Philippines economy. Also, the CP Group, one of the largest food companies in the world, will be expanding its presence in the Philippines while Filipino companies like San Miguel Corp., Universal Robina Corp., and Oishi have invested in Thailand. Then Thai PM Somchai focused on the concluded Memorandum of Understanding on air tourism to promote trade and investments as part of an overall Thailand-Philippines tourism package. Bilaterally or regionally, ASEAN needs solidarity to combat the crisis. This was the message sent out by its two most vocal advocates, Thailand and the Philippines.

CHAPTER 22

A Shift in Power Center?

In the 1990s when Southeast Asia was infected by a bout of the 1997 Asian financial crisis which incapacitated most of the Newly Industrializing Economies (NIEs) (except Hong Kong which was single-handedly kept afloat by China) and almost all of the third-tier geese (particularly Thailand and Indonesia which are still recovering from it while Malaysia inoculated itself with a currency peg). But it left the fourth-tier (former socialist CMLV states) relatively untouched and most importantly, the biggest of the fourth-tier member, China, superpumped its economic drive to eventually become the world's latest trillion dollar economy a decade after the financial crisis.

While the economic power of Japan and the four tiger economies of East Asia are already old stories, the rise of China is perhaps the most important tale of this century. In Fareed Zakaria's article in Newsweek "Does the Future Belong to China?", he writes, "Fifteen years ago, Pudong, in east Shanghai, was undeveloped countryside. Today it is Shanghai's financial district, eight times the size of London's new financial district, Canary Wharf… At the height of the Industrial Revolution, Britain was called 'the workshop of the world.' That title surely belongs to China today."

Zakaria states, "It manufactures two thirds of the world's copiers, microwave ovens, DVD players and shoes ... China has grown around 9% a year for more than 25 years, the fastest growth rate for a major economy in recorded history. In that same period it has moved 300 million people out of poverty and quadrupled the average Chinese person's income. And all this has happened, so far, without catastrophic social upheavals. The Chinese leadership has to be given credit for this historic achievement."

1997 gave China a chance to show its newfound strength. One consequence of the 1997 crisis was the acceleration of the integration of Hong Kong into China. Hong Kong returned to China's sovereignty on 1 July 1997. It was during this period that residents of Hong Kong began to appreciate their dependence on China — perhaps for the first time as China backed Hong Kong out of the 1997 Asian financial crisis. Hong Kong's reliance on China also reflects a sea change in the global economy. Hong Kong has also benefited much from this relationship as its currency was argued by commentators to have been sheltered from the worst effects of the 1997 Asian financial crisis as China lent a helping hand to prevent the free-fall of the Hong Kong dollars.

China also upgraded its international and regional profiles. In central Asia, China will work together with the ADB and other parties concerned to contribute to regional economic development and common prosperity in Central Asia, Vice Minister of Finance Li Yong told the 6th Ministerial Conference on Central Asia Regional Economic Cooperation (CAREC) in Dushanbe, in front of some 200 officials or representatives from eight member states and international organizations including the World Bank, the ADB, the IMF and the United Nations Development Program who attended the conference. Li said he hoped that the ADB and other international organizations would provide more funding and technical support for CAREC, an ADB-supported regional cooperation mechanism initiated in 1997.

There should be increased cooperation between CAREC and other organizations including the Shanghai Cooperation Organization, said Li. (CAREC groups together China, Afghanistan, Azerbaijan, Kazakhstan, Kyrgyzstan, Mongolia, Tajikistan and Uzbekistan and focuses on regional initiatives on transport, trade facilitation, trade policy and energy.) CAREC will carry out more than 100 investment and technical assistance projects in 10 years, which will need some US$20 billion. The meeting also approved a transport and trade facilitation strategy, which focuses on the construction of six Eurasian transport lines.

Similarly, Africa is expected to receive more Chinese goodies. Zhou Xiaochuan, governor of the People's Bank of China pledged increased funding for the African Development Fund which funds anti-poverty programs in forty of the continent's poorest nations. In 2006, China also promised to double aid to Africa by 2009, set up a US$5 billion investment fund and provide US$3 billion in loans over the next three years.

Closer to the East Asian region in 1988, Beijing and Vientiane normalized relations, and since the 1997 Asian financial crisis which has economically devastated most of Lao's ASEAN neighbors thus rendering them economically weak, China's economic power in Laos has risen considerably. 1997 marked Laos' economic dependence on Beijing. In 1997, when Laos urged China to help bail out the economy by increasing aid, trade, and investment, China responded positively with a series of bilateral agreements covering economic and technical cooperation, investment and banking, infrastructure development, generous export subsidies and interest-free loans, all of which enabled Laos to stabilize the value of its currency during a crisis in 1998–1999.[1]

Laos then responded positively to this economic friendship. It is a geographic conduit through which Chinese goods from its Southwest provinces can flow into the Thai market and natural resources from Laos including timber, iron ore, copper, gold, and gemstones can be transported to China. According to the *Vientiane Times*, total Chinese investments in Laos from 1988 to 2004 reached $342 million, making it among the top three foreign investors in Laos by 2004.[2] China is now Laos' key to prosperity. Prime Minister Boungnang Vorachit pledged to halve the number of people below the poverty line from two to one million and triple per capita income to $1200–1500 by 2020. In order to achieve these targets Boungnang highlighted the need to expand economic ties with China.[3]

However, China needs to convince the Americans that their rise is not a threat to American economic interests. It has to allay Western suspicions of its motives and the risk of getting bogged down in military and political quagmires of the developing world. China also has to take into consideration its much-vaunted and self-declared status of respecting national sovereignty (a coded message to rebut political interference from Western countries in developing world affairs) and the principle of non-interference which has even given the World Bank, IMF and ADB a run for its money as developing countries turn to China's offer of aid and help with no strings attached. China must also be sensitive of its increasing influence on the US economy. When Chinese central bank governor Zhou Xiaochuan indicated in November 2006 that China would diversify its reserves away from the US dollar, his comments triggered an immediate mild sell-off of the US dollar.

One way to avert problems with the US is through dialogue, specially the Strategic Economic Dialogue (SED). It is a scene reminiscent of the 1980s when the US confronted Japan over the latter's rising economic power which seemingly hurt US economic interests. This time, it is China's turn in the hot seat. The second SED was not just a simple dialogue but, in the words of US Treasury Secretary Henry Paulson, "pivotal to the future of the global economy."

"The SED is a forum to manage that relationship on a long-term strategic basis, for our mutual benefit, and to work towards near-term agreements that build confidence on both sides," said Paulson, also as special envoy of US President George W. Bush. "Our two countries can set a standard and a framework for the rest of the globalized community," he said. "Never before have so many ministers from China gathered in one place in the United States," Paulson said. In fact, half of China's cabinet was in Washington.

But Secretary Paulson is also under pressure to deliver. US Treasury Secretary Henry Paulson, in his opening remarks at the two-day "strategic economic dialogue" meeting, highlighted "persistent trade and financial imbalances", reiterating that Americans were "impatient". At the heart of the impatience was a burgeoning trade deficit that reached US$232 billion in 2006. Impatience was also underlined by American fears of China that has emerged as a global manufacturing power, replacing the United States as the top and primary trading partner for many nations in the world. This has given rise to anti-China sentimentalities in the US Congress.

There has and always been a solution at hand. China wants to spend more in the US, especially to purchase its hi-tech products that China wants badly. Chinese Vice Premier Wu wanted the US to relax its export controls and "reverse the trend of dwindling market share of American high-tech products in China." The Americans disagree with this assessment although they are keen to sell more health care, computer systems, environmental systems and energy products to augment bilateral hi-tech trade.

For the Americans, it is an issue of revaluing the Chinese currency. Many members of the Congress argue that it is the exchange rate between the Chinese currency and the US dollar that gives the Chinese an unfair advantage. Some US Congressmen have even said the yuan should be revalued by up to 40%. Such proposals are controversial even in the US because an upward surge in the Chinese currency would probably equate to a falling dollar (the US dollar has fallen substantially against the world's major currencies, especially those in East Asia) which may not be conducive for the American economy. Since the Chinese government allowed a limited float of the yuan in 2007, the yuan has already gone up by about 5% against the US dollar. The yuan continues to appreciate gradually in blocks of 0.3% to 0.5%.

However, with the outbreak of the global financial crisis, calls for Beijing to revalue the yuan have dampened considerably. This is because many in the world, including the US, is hoping that China can help to shore up the global economy and thus its currency stability is crucial. To meet expectations that China would be a stakeholder in rescuing the global economy, China announced a 4 trillion yuan (US$877 billion) stimulus package to stimulate growth and help avert a global recession. This package is about one-fifth of China's US$3.3 trillion gross domestic product in 1997.[4]

This move is taken less than a week in the second week of November 2008 before Premier Wen Jiabao travels to Washington for talks with global leaders to manage the global financial crisis. This move was instituted to indicate that China can help to stabilize the world economy and boost domestic demand through aggressive fiscal policies. The distribution of the funds involved spending 100 billion yuan for low-rent housing, infrastructure construction in rural areas and building roads, rail lines and airports in the urban areas. Beijing will also approve tax deductions for purchases of fixed assets such as machinery to reduce companies' expenditure by about 120 billion yuan while stimulating investments and the central bank in China has cut its interest rates three times in two months, reducing the one year lending rate to 6.66% by the second week of November 2008.[5]

All these are done in the hope of making up for export decline and loss of manufacturing contracts due to deteriorating conditions in the developed countries; and to combat sagging domestic consumption including its waning property market as well as to reduce the stockpile of unsold new cars which is the highest in four years in September 2008.[6]

From a macro perspective, the current world economic model involves China's willingness to purchase and hold on to the dollars as well as purchase US Treasury Bills from their funds that they had earned from exporting to the US and in the process keeping US interest rates low. This releases money for Americans to spend and they went further to borrow against those homes to release funds to spend even more. Both sides benefited from this.

The global financial crisis and the US subprime crisis has dealt the beginning of an end to this partnership, resulting in high US unemployment, excessive American consumption with lower savings, inability of US to absorb Chinese exports. The current system now requires the Chinese consumers to pick up the slack and start spending, something culturally and financially difficult for the Chinese to do. Without a comprehensive Western-style social, unemployment or health security, Chinese are reluctant to spend. The average Chinese consumer is far lower in per capita salary than their Western counterparts. This may require Americans to instead spend less, study harder, be more productive and invest more.

Being less affected by the global financial crisis thus far and having newfound legitimacy from attention lavished upon China to save the world, Chinese President Hu Jintao brought back into vogue China's developmental system as a model. In his commemorative speech for the thirtieth anniversary of China's reforms, Hu referred to Marxism 34 times in his 18,000-word speech. The important economic features of China's economic model, according to the Chinese Communist Party (CCP), included economic development as the central focus of the Party, stability as the foundation for economic growth, eradication of corruption, balancing public and private ownership.

The Chinese leadership sensed widespread disappointment with the American model of capitalism and wasted no time in reiterating the newfound importance of Marxism and the reinvigoration of state enterprise to overcome what the government perceives as the deficiency of the market mechanism.

The US National Intelligence Council (NIC) drew up the report "Global Trends 2025: A Transformed World" which effectively acknowledged that by 2025 the current unipolar system will be transformed into a multipolar one with the rise of China and India. Its economic and military power would have eroded by then. The report is optimistic when commenting on Asian regionalism, especially the ASEAN+3 mechanism which is seen as a pan-Asian organization that can augment economic integration and insulate the region from global financial turmoil and provide greater say for East Asians at the international bargaining table.

While the rise of China is seen as important for the region, at the same time, East Asia should be concerned about the possible change of power if US power diminishes. US influence has been and is still the premium stabilizing factor in the East Asia as China and India become balancing forces in the region. Reflecting the importance of American financial power and its impact on the region, US's global influence on the market remains the worries of many financial powerbrokers around this region.

Even before the 2008 global economic crisis, rattling the markets is the alleged decline of the New York Stock Exchange and losing its shine to other financial centers. In 2005, the New York Stock Exchange gained only six net new listings and NASDAQ just 14 and in the same year, not one of the ten largest new listings globally was registered in the US. These were certainly causes for worries in the region which was why this became a cover story. Such developments also signify the decline of US power to some.

Of course, the weakness of US power, while real, should not be overplayed. In the media example, it may be instructive to note that American institutions actually own nearly one-third of the London Stock Exchange (LSE). On 20 November 2006, NASDAQ increased its ownership of the LSE to 28.75%. Nevertheless, media perceptions of US losing its shine in the region should be addressed. Even the so-called decoupling of East Asia from the US seems to have been proven wrong in the current bout of financial crisis. During the Christmas festive season in 2008, the inability of American consumers to spend has caused factories in China to close down and Asian economies to cut off 2–3% from their growth rates.[7]

It would be impossible for East Asia to completely insulate itself from the global financial crisis. Jakarta for example has approached Australia, Japan, the World Bank and other official creditors to shore up credit to help Indonesia tide over a projected US$4.4 billion budget deficit in 2009. The rupiah has fallen almost 25% in 2008 and its problem raising funds got Indonesian policymakers worried that Indonesia could be the next victim of the global financial crisis. There has also been a movement of investments from Indonesia to safer and less risky financial instruments such as the US Treasury bonds. The ADB had indicated that it could make US$1 billion available but the exact terms of the package is still being worked out. Indonesia wants more from Japan and World Bank sovereign loans and government to government loan arrangement from Canberra. Canberra had previously loaned Indonesia US$1 billion in the 1997 Asian Financial Crisis.

Meanwhile in China, hundreds of retrenched workers in Zhongtang town, Dongguan, Guangdong province of south China destroyed the offices of a toy factory and clashed with the police on 25 November 2008 after 380 workers were laid off by the Kaida Toy Factory owned by a Hong Kong firm. The riots arose when 2,000 workers gathered to protest the severance pay given to laid-off workers. Amongst them, 500 got heated up and rioted while 1,500 others looked on. They were strong enough to overcome 1,000 police, overturned their vehicles and smashed the windows and computer monitors in the factory.

All these indicate that East Asian countries cannot be complacent as the global financial crisis hits the real economies. Besides financial initiatives, East Asia must also embark on other long-term solutions. Some East Asian countries suggest focusing on non-financial related measures such as an overhaul of business education itself with some focus on history to learn from the past. To prevent an incessant focus on profit-orientation, suggestions are made to introduce the humanities in subjects such as political sciences, business history and psychology to have an element of betterment of society.

What Now?

Private Sector Involvement

Beyond state-to-state free trade arrangements, the private sector from East Asia will probably have a big role to play in the current global financial crisis. After all the East Asian governments have shown their cards on what they can do to prime-pump or encourage spending in their respective economies, the rest is up to the private sector or government-linked firms like Beijing's China Investment Corp to buy up the assets of distressed Western, particularly American banks and to provide capital for Southeast Asian entrepreneurs.

The need for capital and liquidity includes Southeast Asian countries, which are seen as vulnerable to financial crises. Vietnam, for example, has given its approval to HSBC and Standard Chartered to become the first foreign banks to open fully owned subsidiaries in the country. Jakarta, also realizing the potential financial power of the private sector to tide over the global financial crisis, has also removed a regulation that could potentially block Malaysia's Maybank's $2.7 billion takeover of an Indonesian bank. In Northeast Asia, China will also give foreign banks greater access to its bond markets in return for US support for China's membership in the Financial Stability forum, a grouping of central bankers and finance ministers from the developed world.

The Obama Factor

Hope is now placed on the successor to President Bush — Barack Obama has won the US presidential elections and expectations at East Asia are piling high on his presidency. Indonesian President Susilo Bambang Yudhoyono congratulated Barack Obama and hoped the new president will take leadership in tiding the world over global financial crisis. President Yudhoyono also hoped that Obama would continue to boost the economy. Indonesia is particularly hopeful of Obama's leadership as the crisis has affected Indonesia's exports and the rupiah has depreciated sharply against the US dollar. Some indications of incoming Obama's leadership is already on display. He made telephone calls to leaders of Australia, Britain, Canada, France, Germany, Israel, Japan, Mexico and South Korea to discuss the crisis.

The transitional and adjustment periods for the incoming administration might be a little bit too long for comfort for some East Asian countries that are facing imminent challenges in the current crisis. Thus, some of them have taken decisive actions to cope with the effects of the current crisis. For example, South Korea announced on 3 November 2008 a $11 billion package to boost the economy. The government's efforts to pursue business-friendly policies, including a three-year plan to promote foreign investment facilitated the inflow of foreign capital. Other contributors included increased investment from Japan and the European Union, which offset the decline in FDI from the US. The Philippine central bank cut bank reserve requirements by 2 percentage points unexpectedly on 7 November 2008 Friday to pump more liquidity into its banking system.

With Western countries grappling with the fallout of the global financial crisis, Northeast Asia powers Japan, China and Korea are helping the region and the world to lessen some impact of the global financial crisis. The People's Bank of China, China's central bank, amassed an estimated (US$22.7 billion) worth of shares in British companies including Cadbury, HSBC, Unilever, Marks and Spencer and Tesco. Chinese officials have been given orders to deploy US$1.7 trillion of foreign exchange holdings through its four main international offices.

The People's Bank of China's arm State Administration of Foreign Exchange (SAFE) would move 5% of its portfolio into shares (a sum of US$85 billion) making it one of the largest SWFs in the world and an equivalent of just over a month's reserve accumulation of China. The People's Bank of China also announced on 9 November 2008 that it would expend S$877 billion for economic expansion to be used by the end of 2010. Initial spending will be used for low-rent housing, rural infrastructure such as roads, railways and airports. Another ten trillion yuan or S$2.2 trillion is added by provincial governments to build infrastructure such as ports, housing and social spending to offset a sharp drop in demand for its goods by markets such as the US. This was announced on 23 November 2008.

Another China factor in stabilizing the region's and the world's economy is the news that since September 2008, China has become the US government's largest foreign creditor, overtaking Japan, by owning $585 billion worth of US Treasuries. Japan holds $573.2 billion worth in the same period.

Japan is also doing its part to insulate Southeast Asia as much as possible from the global financial crisis. It re-affirmed since 13 October 2008 that it would continue to invest in ASEAN countries to make up for the slowdown in the US and the EU as much as possible. Hiroyuki Ishige, Vice Minister for Economy, Trade and Industry, contin-ued to see ASEAN as a strong production base for the world.

Japan also initiated a cooperative venture known as the "East Asia Industrial Corridor" for ASEAN and China, South Korea, India, Australia, New Zealand as well as Japan to invest in their logistics systems and create new shipment links. This will include the New Delhi–Mumbai and the East–West Economic Corridor for ASEAN countries slated to be completed by 2025.

As for Korea, it is doing its part by remaining stable to keep the regional economy in East Asia and Southeast Asia stable. It is also doing its part in regional coordina-tion and cooperation by maintaining a hotline with the IMF and other financial authorities in major countries such as the US, China and Japan. Given the increased experts of petroleum products and ships by October 2008, the Korean trade balance remains in the black until end 2008. The foreign exchange market is stabilized with the currency swap agreement between Korea and the US on 30 October 2008. Korea's main policy measures are removing the uncertainty factor in its currency and finan-cial markets, expanding fiscal expenditures to sustain jobs in the real economy and to institute measures to help the vulnerable SMEs and the general working population at large.

Supply of liquidity is being increased to banks, securities, firms and asset management firms. On 6 October 2008, the Korean government injected $5 billion in fresh foreign currency credit to local banks through the Export–Import Bank of Korea. On 18 October 2008, South Korea allocated an extra $30 billion to help banks, businesses and currency market to stabilize. Out of this, a sum of $20 billion will be provided for small and medium-sized exporters through the state-run Korea Exim Bank while the government will provide another $10 billion into the won-dollar currency swop market. The latter policy is utilized to focus on securing liquidity by increasing currency swap deals. For household lending, the government is encouraging long-term loans and providing credit recovery support to reduce the burden of debt payment for borrowers in the lowest income brackets.

The Korea government injected 14 trillion won into the state budget to retain jobs. It boosted domestic demand with one trillion won in public corporation investment centered on the stabilization of people's livelihood such as support for SMEs and small business owners, spending three billion won on tax cuts in the hope of expanding investment by private sectors and implementing fiscal expenditures earlier than scheduled (50% in the first half of 2008 and around 60% in the first six months of 2009).[1] The Korean government will also prevent a slowdown in real estate and construction by easing excessive regulations imposed upon reconstruction of buildings and real estate, resale restrictions will also be relaxed and tax exemption expanded for local housing as well as lift regulations regarding land, environment and labour.

On 31 October 2008, the Korean government initiated its Guarantee Program where 18 domestic banks, including their branches operating in overseas markets, were provided with a government guarantee and foreign currency debts issued or borrowed by domestic banks between 20 October 2008 and 30 June 2009 will be guaranteed by the government effective for three years as to the payment obligations due and payable on or before 30 June 2012. The limit of the amount of the government guarantee will be $100 billion in total and the Minister of Strategy and Finance may adjust the limit of the guarantee amount for each bank within the total guarantee if necessary and the guarantee amount for each bank will not be less than $100 million.[2]

Unity in Adversity

East Asia also needs to work with Europe to come out of this crisis. Asian and European leaders are realizing the severity of the financial crisis and trying to rally together to fight the scourge. The Asia–Europe Meeting (ASEM), opened on 17 October 2008, was an attempt to minimize the differences between Asian and European leaders in tackling the crisis.

The scale of this meeting is significant as it covers two-thirds of world trade and 60% of global output. Southeast Asia also took its opportunity to exchange views with the global powers of EU, Tokyo and Beijing. Consensus amongst the 45 states from different continents is not easy but a united front is needed to cope with the global

financial crisis. Even a hint of this unity will help to contribute to restoring confidence in the market.

As the White House braced the US public for a sharp
rise in layoffs and unemployment, Southeast Asia and
Europe hopes that China and India will step up in the
crisis and spur world growth. ASEAN's European counterparts are also doing their part. France unveiled plans
for a 100 billion euro (128 billion dollar) sovereign wealth
fund to protect key industries from turmoil. French
President Nicolas Sarkozy's main goal in Beijing was to
win Asian support for his ambitious financial reform
plans and to completely reshape the global economic
structure to replace the Bretton Woods system that
has governed international finance since the end of
World War II, with the Washington summit to kick off
the process.

ASEAN countries had already met with their Northeast
Asian counterparts just before the ASEM meeting in
the ASEAN+3 meeting. More importantly, ASEAN met
with Japan, China and South Korea to beef up a regional
mechanism for emergency financial support. Political
unity even in the micro sense is important as Thailand
and Cambodia attended, despite their sputtering border
dispute.

However, analysts say that, despite the multilateral
grandeur, it is more likely that the Southeast Asian and
East Asian states would continue to rely on quiet and
polite bilateral diplomacy to work towards a regional
solution. The meeting runs against some pretty gloomy
scenarios as outlooks from US, European and Japanese
companies are unlikely to give many grounds for optimism. But the urgency of such multilateral summits

and coordinated actions is increasing by the day as already Ukraine, Belarus and Pakistan have appealed for assistance from the IMF. The world needs all the unity it can get.

There are calls for Asian countries to speak up at the G20 global summit in Washington DC in mid-2008. Major East Asian economies like China and Japan will be attending the summit. Some have called for Asian countries not to scold or blame the West for the crisis. At the same time, they should not miss this opportunity to have their voices heard as well. They are urged to let their ideas be circulated in a possible attempt to re-engineer the global financial system. Some have called East Asian to make a clear stance that they are for free trade and not increased protectionism in an attempt to pressure the US not to impose inward-looking measures to protect their workers.

APEC

There are also calls to take this opportunity to bind East Asian economies closer to the US and not further. This can be done by utilizing the Asia Pacific Economic Cooperation (APEC) forum since the US will be hosting it two years later, after Singapore and Japan. East Asia can also ride on the momentum created by the US's interest on a Pacific-4 trade agreement linking Singapore, Brunei, Chile and New Zealand.

State leaders, senior bureaucrats and businessmen gathering in Peru for the APEC annual meeting with one agenda on the mind: the global financial crisis. APEC countries make up 60% of the world's economy and allows smaller countries (especially those not in the G20) like

Brunei to make their voices heard through the institu-
tionalized structure of meetings, committees and action
groups. Moves towards an APEC Free Trade Area (FTA)
were first catalyzed in Bogor Indonesia in 1994 and an
APEC committee is now studying this possibility by
examining what should be considered as elements of a
high quality FTA, including whether APEC will meet
the Bogor Goals for free and open trade amongst indus-
trialized APEC economics by 2010 and developing
economies by 2020.

High quality in terms of FTA is benchmarked by the
gold standards of the US–Singapore FTA. A Comprehensive
Trans-Pacific Strategic Economic Partnership Agreement
now links the Pacific Rim countries of Chile, Singapore
Brunei and New Zealand, all small players with big ambi-
tions of tearing down tariffs. This P-4 groups has great
potential for expansion with bigger boys coming in,
including the US, Australia, Vietnam, Peru.

G-20

As world leaders of twenty countries (G-20) representing
85% of the world's economy gathered in Washington to
discuss about the global financial crisis, one thing that
they agreed on is a joint approach to tackle the economy.
The inclusion of developing countries have been an innovative and welcomed push to get more developing countries involved in saving the world economy.

But, a divide has broken out between the Europeans
and the Americans. Europeans want more state control
over market and giving government regulators cross-
border-cross-boundary powers while the US wants to keep
regulation within national boundaries. The Europeans

have proposed setting up colleges of supervisors that will meet regularly to share and exchange information about global bank operations across borders. They also hope to expand the membership of the financial stability forum group of finance ministers and central bankers to include developing countries membership (especially large developing economies like China and Brazil).

The Americans oppose such proposals. With such early deadlocks, it is likely that Japan, China and countries like Saudi Arabia may end up as possible tipping points for any disagreements. Japan, for example, is taking the lead in providing $100 billion to the IMF and is pushing other countries to contribute similar amounts to do the same. But Asian countries are also getting nervous about rising calls for protectionism within the developed world.

The EU has also slapped anti-dumping duties on Chinese-made candles and non-alloy steel products of up to 60% that accounted for $380.6 million of the EU market, worth US$1 billion in 2007. Extra duties of up to 50% will be levied on non-alloy steel wire products from China for half a year starting from November 2008. One of Southeast Asia's G20 representative, Indonesia, meanwhile has called for a strategic partnership with the US to confront challenges in the 21st century and focuses on equal partnership and common interests as elements of US-developing world relations.

Coping with Challenges

Coping Strategies in East Asia

Asia's potential to contribute to resolving the current financial crisis is huge with purchasing power parity terms making up 35% of the world's GDP compared to US and the EU's 20% respectively. The continent has also been contributing to 50% of the world's growth in recent year. The region holds one-third of the world's central bank reserves.

China started to accumulate dollar-denominated assets in the mid-1990s and they now make up approximately 70% of its reserves. To help US and itself, it cannot rock the boat by divesting its US holdings to protect the value of their own dollar holdings. China's exposure to the Lehman Minibonds is small, just $700 million. According to EU's Maastricht Treaty, a country with a debt amounting 60% of its GDP and a current account deficit of 3% is not in danger if its GDP growth is close to 5% and China's debt in 2007 was 25% of its GDP with a current account surplus of $400 billion (15% of its GDP) with economic growth of 11.4% in 2007.

China People's Bank decreased interest rate in early December 2008 and for the first time, China participated in coordinated global interest rate cuts on 8 October 2008. Its stimulus package, equivalent to 15% of its GDP is the largest one that any country has ever taken in response to the global financial crisis.

China's local government also added an additional ten trillion yuan (S$2.2 trillion) to stimulate its economy, including three trillion yuan invested in Yunnan province and 2.3 trillion in Guangdong province. With the release of capital into the local areas, the infrastructure, construction and machinery sectors will benefit, banks get help from the expansion of loan volumes which helps to lessen the margin squeeze resulting from low interest rates and the utility sector can profit from the demand for power with the increased infrastructure and construction works. Other local level initiatives include the Beijing city government offering a subsidy to firms giving jobs to retrenched workers.

Its state media has also launched propaganda to encourage domestic spending and instill confidence in the domestic economy. In addition, instead of hiding bad news about labour unrest and the impact of the global financial crisis on the Chinese economy, Chinese state media has increased reporting of protests over land, labour and investment issues to manage the impact of negative news by acknowledging and publicizing it to prevent excessive rumour-mongering. Market regulators also disciplined Chinese trading houses to avoid excessive overseas speculation, limit their activity to legitimate hedging.

Patriotism was also mobilized in South Korea in the second week of October 2008 when President Lee Myung-bank discouraged the hoarding of dollars and encouraged consumers and companies to exchange dollars and other foreign currencies for the Korean won. This is a reenactment of the 1997–1998 appeal by the Korean government to buy local cars and donate gold to the central bank.

In the weekend between 15–16 November 2008, Japan released up to $100 billion to the IMF as financial help to emerging economies and invested $2 billion in a new World Bank fund to help recapitalize banks in smaller emerging markets. Domestically, Japan's PM Taro Aso announced on 12 December 2008 an extra S$165 billion stimulus package to help the Japanese economy through tax breaks and public financing and another 13 trillion to prop up financial markets. This piggybacks on a 27 trillion yen stimulus package announced in October 2008, which focused on expanded credits for small businesses and a cash payout to every household to stimulate spending.

Mitsubishi UFJ Financial Group (MUFG) has purchased 20% of Morgan Stanley, Nomura Holdings bought up Lehman operations in Asia, Europe and the Middle East, giving them access to new markets and growth potential in the long run. Morgan Stanley also benefits from this by gaining access to MUFG's $1.1 trillion in bank deposits in exchange for MUFG's representation on Morgan's board and business tie-ups. Morgan will also have access to $15 trillion personal financial assets in Japan, about $8 trillion of which are in bank deposits. Sumitomo Mitsui also injected several hundred billion yen in Goldman. MUFG also laid out $3.5 billion to buy the remaining 35% stake in UnionBanCal, making its ownership of the bank total. Up till 25 September 2008, overseas acquisitions by Japanese banks and other financial institutions made up a total of $12.5 billion.

Weak Points of Asia

Challenges in Vietnam

The global financial crisis has opened a divide between conservatives and reformers/progressives within the Vietnamese Communist Party. Before the outbreak of the US subprime and global financial crises, Vietnam was already facing tremendous challenges with heightened inflation (around 22%), sizable current account deficit (about 19% of GDP in 2008) and decreasing foreign investments. The global financial crisis has added two more challenges — less remittances from overseas Vietnamese and a decline in tourism coupled with foreign exchange shortfall.

The Vietnamese response so far has been to follow global applications of fixes, including a $1 billion stimulus package that started on 2 December 2008 and corporate tax reduction announced on 12 December 2008. Such measures have not come easy. Vietnamese PM Nguyen Tan Dung had to pit his expansionist reformist/progressive group against conservatives like Party Secretary general Nong Duc Manh who is more in favour of slower sustainable growth to root out pollution, inflation and corruption, picking on such sentiments rising within the middle class.

The fallout from PM Tan Dung's declining political legitimacy posed by slower growth is real. As they are in the majority, the Conservatives are using their numbers in the party politburo and central committee to exert their influence. In 2007, the conservatives rejected some of PM Dung's appointees to the Cabinet, use their power base in the Information and Communications Ministry to arrest journalists investigating corruption in the Transport

Ministry and mobilized the Ministry of Public Security to ignore his calls for corruption investigation. They also instigated the unprecedented holding of three central committee meetings to discuss political issues and transfer the power to run Vietnamese economy from the Cabinet to the politburo. PM Tan Dung's crucial allies, the Finance Minister and the Bank Governor are now increasingly isolated.

PM Tan Dung's rapid economic growth promises are increasingly difficult to sustain as Vietnam's growth slows down along with the global economic downturn. He has a tenuous hold on power and can only depend on Vietnamese comparative advantages like a young population (75% under 35 years old), English language fluency amongst its workforce and high literacy rates amongst its population to keep those investments coming.

Challenges in Japan

Critics have countered that the October 2008 stimulation package is not enough because the main components of that supplementary budget are cash handouts and lower expressway tolls while job creation programs, clearly needed during difficult economic times, were not the main pillar of that package. Others consider this initiative as a gimmicky populist policy by the ruling party LDP (Liberal Democratic Party) for the upcoming lower house elections.

While popular, they counter, the stimulus package may result in bloated expenditures and debt, focusing for the time being on economic stimulation while neglecting improvement of the fiscal condition. The central government will be forced to issue 33.294 trillion yen in new central government bonds, the first time in four years that an initial budget proposal has had new bond issuance in excess of 30 trillion yen.[1] This will make it difficult for Japan to achieve a primary balance surplus in fiscal 2011.

In the currency and interest rate aspects, the Bank of Japan (BOJ) lowered its interest rate from 0.3–0.1% on 19 December 2008. This move was forced by the steep fall of the dollar to a 13-year low against the yen on the third week of December after the US rate cut which propelled many investors dumped the dollar for yen and other currencies. An appreciating yen hurts Japan's export-oriented economy as it limited companies' profits when converted into yen. But, on the other hand, pushing interest rates even closer toward zero would discourage banks from lending. This central bank concern expressed through BOJ Governor Masaaki Shirakawa probably explains why it reduced the rate to 0.1% instead of zero.

To combat the fear of further liquidity crunch, BOJ supports the credit markets where companies raise funds by launching a new, temporary program to buy commercial paper, a critical short-term debt instrument for businesses as a countermeasure. Besides the unwanted effect of tightening up the credit markets, others have criticized the move towards lower BOJ interest rate for compromising the independence of the central banks as the lowered interest rates is perceived as a consequence of undue pressure from cabinet members for political reasons.

Japan's economic fallout from the global financial crisis deepened by Christmas Day 2008. First data released on 22 December 2008 indicated that Toyota would post its first operating loss (150 billion yen) in 71 years against the backdrop where Japan's exports plunged 26.7% in November 2008 compared to one year ago, a new record in Japan's industrial history. Shipments of cars and electronics to the US decreased by yet another record-breaking number — 34%. The November 2008 trade deficit of 223.4 billion yen was much larger than the October deficit of 67.7 billion yen, reversing a surplus of 784.4 billion yen one year ago.

Japan's challenge in managing the financial crisis is also as political as it is economic. Alongside the challenges posed by the global economic downturn, Japan is also facing political uncertainty domestically. With the support rate for PM Aso and his Cabinet plunging to 25.5% in early December 2008, Aso's three month old administration is struggling before the general election deadline in September 2009.[2] Aso's biggest problem is coping with internal dissent.

Heavyweights like former LDP Vice President Taku Yamasaki, former Secretaries General Koichi Kato and Hidenao Nakagawa, and former Chief Cabinet Secretary Yasuhisa Shiozaki are already distancing themselves from Aso. The biggest political setback for Aso was internal dissent by ex-administrative reform minister Yoshimi Watanabe who sided with the opposition DPJ in a recent bill submitted to the Diet on Christmas Eve urging Aso to dissolve the Lower House.

It is going to be a tough year for Aso with all these political problems. In the next few months, he must obtain the Japanese parliament Diet's approval for the second supplementary budget for fiscal 2008, the fiscal 2009 budget, and legislations containing the economic measures to fight rising unemployment and economic downturn.

Challenges in China

Domestically, Premier Wen Jiabao has made job creation for graduates and laid-off migrant workers returning to their villages as the top priority in his administration. According to the Chinese Academy of Social Sciences (CASS), only 70% of the 5.6 million graduates were able to find jobs in 2008. This will be complicated by the entry of 6.5 million graduate job-seekers in 2009. As for migrant workers (210 million in all), up to nine million of them have gone back to their hometowns after being laid off by China's industries in the South whose production has been affected by the slowdown in the export markets and the global financial crisis.

China's government has also been flamed by angry web bloggers for using its hard-earned savings to bail out and invest in loss-incurring US investments. This will make it more difficult in the future for Beijing to continually cushion the US downturn. The East Asian economies with surpluses — China, HK, Japan and South Korea — have aging populations that will decrease their savings rates in the long run. The aging population will pressure dwindling workforce in these countries.

After the G20 meeting, different governments around the world are implementing strategies according to their national conditions to meet the needs of the crisis. East Asia is also gearing up to retain as many jobs as possible in this global economic climate. In Japan's case, demand for Japanese cars had fallen overseas, forcing the Japanese carmaker giant Toyota to slash its forecast earnings in 2008 to less than one-third of the previous year. Japan's carmakers based in the US even had to offer interest-free loans to up its sagging car sales. Analysts in Nomura for example has urged the government to boost government spending on research and development (e.g. in fossil fuel alternatives), medical healthcare and education on top of the classic infrastructure building to boost domestic consumption. Others have suggested cutting corporate tax and rectifying problems in Japan's national pension system.

East Asia will face challenges from the financial crisis as it deepens. The crisis' sudden withdrawal of investment by foreign investors, the increased cost of capital, slower growth and the decreasing aid for development programs will put on strain on the region. All these factors may affect lower skilled labor and remittances for economies like the Philippines. Cutting aid for the poor in times of crisis, especially a deepening one like this, will cause even greater distress for the poor. Better social safety nets within the framework of spending stimulation by the government may serve the dual purpose of aiding the poor while combating the crisis at the same time.

Developing an East Asian Business Ethos[a] by Ho Kwon Ping, 30 September 2008

Events of the past two weeks have been breath-taking and doubtless, more shocks will be coming. Some people have said this September 15 is the financial equivalent of September 11 and that this is a War on Wall St, compared to the war on terror. If a war analogy is apt, then I'd like to recast Churchill's famous words:

> *"Indeed, never in human history have* **so many** *lost* **so much** *due to the irresponsible actions of* **so few.***"*

For me, there is in particular a strange sense of déjà vu, an uncomfortable convergence of past and present.

To re-discover requires us to first, recall the past. Let us recall then, that exactly ten years ago the Asian financial crisis raged like wildfire through the region.

Corporates, banks, even governments — one domino after another collapsed due to imprudent borrowings, poor

---

[a] Excerpts of the speech by Mr. Ho Kwon Ping at the Singapore Venture Capital Association Gala Dinner on 30 September 2008. He is the Chairman of Singapore Management University, Executive Chairman of Banyan Tree Holdings and Chairman of MediaCorp. Reprinted with permission. Copyright © Ho Kwon Ping.

corporate governance and crony capitalism. Southeast Asia has still to fully recover from the aftershocks of that crisis.

Today, history repeats itself, but halfway around the world. And the fiercest critics then — the Western, and particularly American, banks — are now having to eat their own words. The very institutions which, by self-righteously blocking bailouts of distressed Asian banks, in order to pick them up at fire-sale prices, are now tasting their own medicine.

As the battle between Main Street and Wall Street builds up in America and the rest of the world watches with the transfixed fascination of a deer staring into the head-lights of a car about to run it down, it would perhaps be forgivable to indulge in some bitter gloating. Unfortunately, there isn't much to gloat about. Southeast Asia may have recovered economically from its financial crisis, but it is mired in other, perhaps even more intractable problems.

As China basks in its post-Olympics after-glow, and other countries move glacially but nevertheless inexorably towards the light of social harmony and reconciliation, the two geographic anchors and arguably most stable societies of South East Asia — Thailand and Malaysia — are at best receding backwards, and at worse, spiraling towards schisms which, once they tear the social fabric apart, will be hard to repair.

Indonesia has at least not disintegrated Yugoslavian style, but its per capita GDP, once double that of China in the 1980's, is now one-third below China's. It's poverty level has not improved in 20 years.

Ten years after the worst crisis since World War Two to engulf South East Asia — the financial melt-down of 1997 — this region has still not resolved its fundamental socio-political problems. Beneath the romantic veneer of diversity which I had innocently and naively celebrated as a youth, are dark and unresolved racial, religious, and class tensions which have only been papered over by economic growth.

Thailand is not just facing the usual musical chairs of coups, counter-coups, and revolving-door governments. Thaksin's unprecedented, Latin American style of populism opened up sharp divisions in Thai society which has unfortunately also dragged the previously apolitical monarchy into the fray, albeit still discreetly. Not since the 1970s has Thailand been so fundamentally polarized.

Polarization is also the common theme running through Malaysian politics. The politics of multi-racial accommodation, with its delicate power-sharing between the politically dominant Malays and economically dominant Chinese communities, has, despite abuses and failures, worked well for 50 years. But as with all founding parties, hubris, corruption and complacency has haunted Malaysia's ruling party.

If I am unduly harsh, it is perhaps because I have loved and believed too much in this region and its promise; this collection of diverse religions, cuisines, music, art and people, sandwiched between the two great and ancient civilizations of India and China, yet preserving in each of the ten nations of ASEAN, their own individual identities — and of course, idiosyncrasies.

In population size, ASEAN compares with the European Union. Indonesia alone rivals the USA in population.

But while the EU has successively demolished one barrier after another to achieve real integration in trade, monetary union, cross-border people movement, and now increasingly even a common foreign and defense policy — ASEAN prefers a talk-fest, full of sound and fury, signifying nothing.

ASEAN largely succeeded as a bulwark against the expansion of communism via Vietnam in the 1970's, but its record as an economic entity has been little short of dismal. You would not discern this from the lofty communiqués issued after each ASEAN ministerial or summit meeting.

But aside from self-congratulatory diplomats, ASEAN has not resolved a single major intra-regional crisis, whether it be Burma or the Indonesian haze or the tsunami aftereffects, nor launched any break-through economic or political initiatives.

The much vaunted ASEAN Consensus is essentially a euphemism for debilitating procrastination and inaction. The ASEAN Charter, devised to give some teeth to the organization and which should be ratified by all member states by this December, looks like it may well fail, with several important signatories again balking.

My remarks are tinged with frustration at the many lost opportunities for true ASEAN integration, and with anger at the politicians who have failed the test of history. Southeast Asia could have been so different, its potential remains barely tapped.

For businessmen, venture capitalists and private equity fund managers, the dynamism and potential of Southeast Asia provides many opportunities for those intrepid, shrewd and patient enough to find them. One consolation is that this time round, our financial systems remain relatively robust. But if we succeed as businessmen, it will be in spite of, not because of, the weak, self-serving and divided political leadership in our region.

* * * * *

The paucity of leadership is at least something both Southeast Asia and the USA share in common. But whereas both political and corporate leadership are sorely lacking in the US, in Asia there is a genuine, though realistically slim chance, for corporate leaders to show leadership in devising an alternative to the Wall Street ethos.

The globalization of capitalism in the past half-century has resulted in two major socio-cultural variants. The dominant variant — American capitalism — was built on very high income inequality as the incentive for risk taking and wealth creation. Its flaws were, of course, recently exposed.

As one observer noted, the subprime crisis and its aftermath, the humiliating bailout, has done to US leadership in financial markets what Guantanamo Bay and Abu Ghraib has done to the US moral high ground in human rights.

The second variant is Euro-capitalism. The European model of capitalism, influenced by democratic socialist tendencies after WWII, ultimately produced welfare capitalism with its stifling effect on individual initiative and entrepreneurship. It has not been a particularly inspiring alternative to Wall Street as a recipe for becoming a millionaire quickly, but it has at least proven to be less socially disruptive and therefore possibly more sustainable.

But the real issue here is not the survival nor even well-being of American-style capitalism. It is whether, after almost fifty years of virtually unchallenged supremacy, American capitalism should be the unquestioned model for a newly resurgent East Asia. And if not, what alternative model can East Asian thought leaders devise, drawing upon their own unique history and socio-cultural heritage?

Most commentaries on the source of the current crisis dwell on regulatory failures or excessive risk-taking, but they all fail to situate the analysis within a human context — that it was people who did all these things, and that people always function within a larger socio-cultural context. And people, as any behavioral psychologist will certify, respond strongly to incentives.

Many critics have correctly focused on the perverse pay structure of Wall Street — a highly skewed risk-reward system gone awry — as the root cause of today's problems.

Perverse and highly inequitable compensation structures are not only morally objectionable, but more importantly, they are the obvious symbols of a society's value system. And quaint though it may sound, values do matter even in a highly sophisticated financial system.

Successive financial crises have proven one consistent point — regulation by itself cannot prevent excessive speculation or collusive behavior. Greed fuels any speculative boom and aggravates a bust, but it can only be reined in, not by regulation alone, but by a moral framework, the value system of the entire society, within which business is practiced.

As East Asia emerges as a major economic region, it should not simply adopt the American nor European models, but create its own alternative, rooted in its own, traditional value systems.

The common, recurring socio-ethical tradition of East Asia is its communitarian, family-focused, webs of mutual obligations. This communitarian characteristic of East Asian culture can, if thoughtfully enhanced, nurtured and developed, replace the highly individualistic, Darwinian ethos of American capitalism, or the state-welfarist tendencies of Euro-capitalism.

China and Japan are the two leading examples of neo-Confucian culture. Much of the communitarian ethic of Japan, derided by Western critics as overly consensual and conservative, can actually be re-learnt by China, which has perhaps in its headlong rush towards wealth, imbibed the worst of the American ethic of individualism, and forgotten its Confucian traditions.

Of course, critics will argue that a neo-Confucian capitalism equates to crony capitalism, as the 1997 Asian financial crisis highlighted. They have a point, but the flaws of East Asian culture do not negate the need to develop a socio-cultural alternative to the Wall Street ethos.

Instead, it only makes more urgent, the need for East Asian thought leaders to engage in the debate as to what a neo-Confucian capitalism actually means. We need to refine and redefine, neo-Confucian values in our own corporate lives.

What other roles can the financial investment community play in this shift of global economic power East-wards, to create a sustainable and perhaps more values-based form of capitalism?

To the extent that bankers have been financial intermediaries in any society, they can also be social intermediaries, helping to shape opinions and values. Just as "Greed is good" was a Wall Street ethic which insidiously permeated all US consumer behaviour, perhaps our financial services practitioners here can help make *"Collective is cool"*, an alternative ethic for East Asia!

The sheer dynamism, ingenuity, and innovation which drove Wall Street can be channeled for better purposes.

One columnist rejoiced that finally, bright minds can be channeled to useful things like making better mousetraps or finding cancer cures, rather than just ways to enrich themselves.

There will certainly be lots of ex-bankers around. Half of America's 8500 banks and one-third of its 10,000 hedge funds will fold. If we assume that each of these 7500 failed or soon-to-fail institutions will eventually result in just say 1000 professionals out of jobs, that's already 7.5 million people. Add in Europe and elsewhere and you get maybe ten or more million bonus-rich but out-of-work bright minds, licking their wounds while rewriting their resumes.

Investment bankers have, collectively, some of the highest intellects in any field of endeavor. They now need to channel that brain power towards helping to solve other people's real problems, rather than tend to their own wants.

They can apply their intellects and energy for example, towards creating a more sophisticated and vibrant social enterprise sector, or towards the problems of carbon trading. They can help to redirect global capital pools, such as sovereign wealth funds, to where they are most needed, and to diminish political barriers in places where they are not wanted.

They can help, in the best tradition of venture capital, to fund socially useful start-ups in new fields such as alternative energy. They can promote and guide Asian entrepreneurs aspiring towards the global stage.

Because in the good times financial services attracted the best and brightest young minds, and many of these are now burnt out and depressed, wondering quite legitimately what it was all about and was it all worth it — leaders such as yourselves need to create a new vision other than financial rewards, to motivate your younger colleagues.

East Asia, caught in the throes of its own greedy, headlong thrust towards wealth, certainly needs an ethos constructed from its own traditional values system. It is perhaps ironic that while America was being humiliated by its financial meltdown, China was also on front page news for the widening scandal over tainted milk. Neither society nor culture can claim the moral high ground nor monopoly on selfish behavior and greed.

But to the extent that East Asia society is clearly more communitarian than individualistic in outlook and values, there is a chance that East Asian capitalism can avoid some — certainly not all — of the pitfalls of American capitalism which led to the debacles today. We laugh at the many values-creating mass campaigns of Singapore and China — the anti-littering campaigns, the courtesy campaigns, the endless exhortations to create communitarian values and collective good behavior, and Western cynics deride these as social engineering.

But we ignore at our peril, the need to pro-actively create an entire values system rooted in the symbols and fables of our own cultural traditions, which can become the ethical foundation of an East Asian, neo-Confucian capitalism.

But even if an East Asian model of capitalism does indeed emerge, we should not think that this will prevent future bubbles and scandals. Greed and selfishness can only be *mitigated* by culture and values, not eradicated. But in an imperfect world — and indeed, only Communism ever contemplated an utopian perfection — a little *less* imperfection will go a long way.

It is perhaps even a little comforting to know that imperfection is the human condition and that mankind has known how to blow bubbles since time immemorial.

There have been over 60 major bubbles since the first recorded bubble 400 years ago in 1622, when the Holy Roman Empire debased its currency, triggering the equivalent of a modern banking panic. The 1637 tulip boom-and-bust in Holland, when a single tulip was worth more than a house, or the 1720 South Sea bubble, are only a few of the more exotic crashes.

The only long term way to achieve a sustainable balance between fear and greed — the two drivers of capitalism — is to change a society's entire reward system, and this can only be done with the way society views itself. Barack Obama got it right when he said that the US has lost "its sense of shared prosperity".

It is the *shared* sense of prosperity which is at the very heart of neo-Confucian capitalism, and which East Asia needs to rediscover as the root of its success and the inspiration for its future. As thought leaders and social intermediaries, the onus on you is particularly heavy, and yet potentially inspiring.

And for divided, disunited Southeast Asia, it can perhaps find solace in the recognition that civilizations take decades, if not centuries, to rise or fall. There is still time for this region to catch up with Europe and East Asia.

Notes

Chapter 1

1   Paulson, HM Jr (2008). Facing one challenge at a time, *International Herald Tribune,* 19 November 2008.
2   Ritholtz, B (2008). Big Bailouts, Bigger Bucks, 25 November 2008, http://www.ritholtz.com/blog/2008/11/big-bailouts-bigger-bucks/
3   Dymski, G and R Pollin (1994). *New Perspectives in Monetary Macroeconomic: Explorations in the Tradition of Hyman P. Minsky.* Ann Arbor: University of Michigan Press.
4   What next?, *The Economist,* 20 September 2008, pp. 13–14.

Chapter 2

1   Lopez, RS (1976). *The Commercial Revolution of the Middle Ages, 950–1350.* Cambridge: Cambridge University Press. Finer, SE (1997). *The History of Government, Volumes 2–3.* Oxford: Oxford University Press.
2   Roberts, JM (1996). *A History of Europe.* Oxford: Helicon.
3   Braudel, F (1985). *Civilization and Capitalism Volume 2 — The Wheels of Commerce.* London: Fontana Press.
4   Schumpeter, J (1934). *The Theory of Economic Development.* Boston: Harvard University Press, p. 74.
5   Keynes, JM (1936). *The General Theory of Employment, Interest and Money.* London: MacMillan.

Dymski, G and R Pollin (eds.) (1994). *New Perspectives in Monetary Macroeconomic: Explorations in the Tradition of Hyman P. Minsky.* Ann Arbor: University of Michigan Press.

6 Sylla, R (2004). Hamilton and the Federalist financial revolution, 1789–1795, *The New York Journal of American History,* pp. 32–39.

7 Drucker, P (1999). Innovate or Die, *The Economist,* 23 September.

8 *Ibid.*

9 *Ibid.*

10 McKenney, JL, RO Mason and DG Copeland (1997). Bank of America: The Crest and Trough of Technological Leadership, *MIS Quarterly,* 21(3), pp. 321–353.

Chapter 3

1 Bagehot, W. *Lombard Street: A Description of the Money Market,* http://www.gutenberg.org/etext/4359.

2 Don't get depressed, it's not 1929, *Newsweek,* 27 November 2008.

3 Carroll, C (2009). Banks and Turtles, *Financial Times,* 20 January.

4 Pollin, R and G Dymski (1994). The costs and benefits of financial instability: big government capitalism and the Minsky Paradox, in Dymski, Gary and Pollin, Robert.

5 *Ibid.*

6 *Ibid,* p. 385.

Chapter 4

1 *The Economist,* 29 November 2008, p. 85.

2 Lim, MMH (2008). Old wine in a new bottle: subprime mortgage crisis — causes and consequences, *The Levy Economics Institute, Working Paper No: 532* http://www.levy.org/pubs/wp_532.pdf.

3   Taming the beast, *The Economist*, 11 October 2008, p. 11.

4   Giving credit where it is due, *The Economist*, 8 November 2008, p. 14.

5   *Ibid*, p. 8.

6   Taming the beast, p. 18.

7   Kling, A (2008). Main Street vs. Wall Street, *The American* October 3, http://www.american.com/archive/2008/october-10-08/main-street-vs.wall-street

8   Buffett warns on investment 'time bomb', BBC News, 4 March 2003, http://news.bbc.co.uk/2/hi/business/2817995.stm.

9   Drucker, P (1999). Innovate or Die, *The Economist*, 23 September.

Chapter 5

1   Benston, GJ and Kaufman, GG (1995). Is the banking and payments system fragile? *Journal of Financial Services Research*, 9, 209–240.

2   Drucker, P (1999). Innovate or Die, *The Economist*, 23 September.

Chapter 6

1   Lim, MMH (2008). Old wine in a new bottle: subprime mortgage crisis — causes and consequences, *The Levy Economics Institute, Working Paper No: 532* http://www.levy.org/pubs/wp_532.pdf.

2   *Ibid*.

3   Kregel, J (2008). Minsky's cushions of safety: systematic risk and the crisis in the U.S. subprime mortgage market, *Public Policy Brief*, 93, The Levy Economics Institute of Bard College.

4   Eichengreen, B (1999). *Toward a New International Financial Architecture: A Practical Post-Asia Agenda*, Washington, DC: Institute of International Economics.

5 Dymski, G and R Pollin (1994). *New Perspectives in Monetary Macroeconomics: Explorations in the Tradition of Hyman P. Minsky*. Ann Arbor: University of Michigan Press.

6 Foreign exchange market, http://en.wikipedia.org/wiki/ Foreign_exchange_market, accessed on 21 January 2009.

7 Eichengreen (1999).

8 Offshore bank, http://en.wikipedia.org/wiki/Offshore_ banking, accessed on 21 January 2009.

9 Krugman, P (2009). *The Return of Depression Economics and the Crisis of 2008*. New York: Norton.

10 Stiglitz, J (2004). *Roaring Nineties*. Penguin Books.

11 Offshore bank, http://en.wikipedia.org/wiki/Offshore_ banking, accessed on 21 January 2009.

Chapter 7

1 Leow, J (2008). China seeks 'fairness', *Asian Wall street Journal*, 7 November 2008.

2 Not even a cat to rescue, *The Economist Online Edition*, 20 April 2006.

3 Davis, B (2008). Nations strive for a single voice on crisis, *Asian Wall Street Journal*, 11 November 2008.

4 Not even a cat to rescue, *The Economist Online Edition*, 20 April, 2006.

5 Leow (2008), *ibid.*

6 President Hu Jintao of China wanted to see a "new international financial order that is fair, just, inclusive and orderly". Indian Prime Minister Manmohan Singh envisaged a new financial "architecture suited to the new challenges and vulnera bilities that have taken place in the economic structure". Source: Dombey, D, K Guha and A Ward (2008). Talks challenge club of rich countries, *Asian Wall Street Journal*, 17 November 2008. A similar message is voiced by the Russian President Dmitry Medvedev. Speaking at the G20 financial summit, he pointed out that the global financial

structures created at the end of the Second World War were now inadequate. "It will be necessary to rebuild the whole international financial architecture, make it open and fair, effective and legitimate". Source: BBC news report Summit pledge to 'restore growth' http://news.bbc.co.uk/2/hi/business/7731139.stm.

Chapter 8

1 Allen, F and D Gale (2007). *Understanding Financial Crisis.* Oxford: Oxford University Press.
2 Dymski, G and R Pollin (1994). *New Perspectives in Monetary Macroeconomics*: *Explorations in the Tradition of Hyman P. Minsky.* Ann Arbor: University of Michigan Press.
3 *Ibid.*
4 Blustein, P (2001). *Chastening: Inside the Crisis that Rocked the Global Financial System and Humbled the IMF.* New York: Public Affairs.
5 Fischer, S (1999). *Need for an International Lender of Last Resort.* Talk delivered to the joint luncheon of the American Economic Association and The American Finance Association, 3 Jan 1999. New York. www.imf.org/external/np/speeches/1999/010399.htm, accessed on 26 December 2008.
6 A system is robust if it can comfortably take small shocks, and it is resilient if it bounces back quickly after the small shocks. If the system fails to do so, then it is fragile.
7 20 September 2008, p. 14.
8 Feldstein, M (1991). The risk of economic crisis: an introduction, in Feldstein, M (ed.) *The Risk of Economic Crisis.* Chicago: University of Chicago Press.
9 Quoted in Dymski, G and R Pollin (1994) *New Perspectives in Monetary Macroeconomics*: *Explorations in the Tradition of Hyman P. Minsky.* Ann Arbor: University of Michigan Press, p. 5.
10 Feldstein (1991). *Ibid.*

Chapter 9

1 Rutterman, PJ (1995). Financial fragility and supervision: a discussion, in Benink, HA (ed.) *Coping with Financial Fragility and Systemic Risk*, Boston: Kluwer Academic Publishers, p. 293.
2 Drucker, P (1999). Innovate or Die, *The Economist*, 23 September.
3 March, J (1994). *A Primer on Decision Making*. New York: The Free Press.
4 Lane, P (2004). Trust me, I'm a banker, *The Economist*, 17 April.
5 Communiqué of Meeting of Ministers and Governors of G-20 countries, Sao Paulo, Brazil, 8–9 November 2008.
6 Drucker (1999), *ibid*.
7 Bowers, S (2008). Wall Street banks in $70bn staff payout, 17 October 2008, http://www.guardian.co.uk/business/2008/oct/17/executivesalaries-banking/print accessed on 29 December 2008.
8 F Bass and R Beamish (2008) AP study finds $1.6B went to bailed-out bank execs, 21 December 2008, http://biz.yahoo.com/ap/081221/executive_bailouts.html?.v=2 accessed on Dec 29, 2008.
9 http://www.guardian.co.uk/business/2008/oct/17/executive-salaries-banking/print
10 Letter to the Editor, *The Economist*, 11 October 2008, p. 20.
11 An angel investor has business experience relevant to a company he is investing in and is committed to adding value to the company. His knowledge and commitment play a part in his wish to earn a good return from his investment.

Chapter 10

1 Krugman, P (2009). *The Return of Depression Economics and the Crisis of 2008*. New York: WW Norton.

Chapter 11

1   Lim, MMH (2008). Old wine in a new bottle: subprime mortgage crisis — causes and consequences, *The Levy Economics Institute, Working Paper No: 532*.

2. Fernandez, L, F Kaboub and Z Tadorova (2008). *On Democratizing Financial Turmoil: A Minskian Analysis of the Subprime Crisis*, Working Paper 548. The Levy Economics Institute of Bard College.

3   Huang, J (2009). Social security crucial to higher consumption, *China Daily*, 15 January 2009, http://www.chinadaily.com.cn/cndy/2009-01/15/content_7398526.htm accessed on 22 January 2009.

4   Minsky, H (1995). Financial factors in the economics of capitalism, *Journal of Financial Services Research*, l(9), pp. 197–208.

Chapter 12

1   Rohwer, J (1996). *Asia Rising*. New York: Simon & Schuster, p. 29.

2   *Ibid*.

3   Holland, T (2001). Don't Count on the Cavalry, *Far Eastern Economic Review*. Hong Kong: FEER, p. 48.

4   *Ibid*.

5   Leary, A (2001). "Toothless Tiger", *Asian Business* Hong Kong: Asian Business, p. 48.

6   Holland (2001), *ibid*.

7   *Ibid*.

8   *Ibid*.

9   Luttwak, E (1999). *Turbo Capitalism*. NY: Harpers Perennial, p. 119.

10 *Ibid*.

11 *Ibid*.

Chapter 13

1 Bulletin, M. "East Asia thrives a decade after crisis" dated 5 April 2007 in Manila Bulletin (downloaded on 6 April 2007), available at http://www.mb.com.ph/BSNS2007040691254.html

2 Rosengard, J (2004). *Fiscalization of the East Asian Financial Crisis,* March 2004, Kennedy School of Government website, available at ksgnotes1.harvard.edu/Research/wpaper.nsf/rwp/RWP04012/$File/rwp04_012_rosengard.pdf, p. 5.

3 *Ibid.*

4 *Ibid*, p. 6.

5 *Ibid*, p. 9.

Chapter 14

1 Kim, SJ (2005). Citibank CEO Warns of 2nd Asian Crisis Due to Slow Reforms, 18 May 2005, *Korea Times*, available at http://times.hankooki.com/lpage/biz/200511/kt2005111822134411910.htm, accessed on 6 April 2007.

2 Rosengard, J (2004). *Fiscalization of the East Asian Financial Crisis,* March 2004, Kennedy School of Government website, available at ksgnotes1.harvard.edu/Research/wpaper.nsf/rwp/RWP04012/$File/rwp04_012_rosengard.pdf, p. 11.

3 *Ibid.*

Chapter 15

1 Luttwak, E (1999). *Turbo Capitalism.* NY: HarpersPerennial, 1999 p. 8.

2 Hill, B *Japan Behind the Lines.* Australia: Sceptre, p. 6.

3 Estabrooks, M (1995). Electronic Technology, *Corporate Strategy, and World Transformation.* USA: Quorum, p. 4.

4 Ministry of Internal Affairs and Communications (MIAC) Statistics Bureau and Statistical Research and Training

Institute, *Chapter 3 Economy* in the MIAC website, available at http://www.stat.go.jp/english/data/handbook/c03cont. htm, accessed on 29 September 2006.

5 The Economist, "Plaza Accord" in the Economist.com website, available at http://www.economist.com/research/Economics/ alphabetic.cfm?LETTER=P, accessed on 29 September 2006.

Chapter 16

1 Teo, E (2001). *SIIA Day 2001 Programme — The International Challenges for Singapore, Friday 2 November 2001 Session 2: The China Factor and ASEAN*. Singapore: SIIA, 2001.

2 CIA Factbook, "Vietnam" in the CIA World Factbook website, available at https://www.cia.gov/library/ publications/the-world-factbook/geos/vm.html, accessed on 17 August 2008.

3 Spencer, M and J Lee (2007). Korea stands firm 10 years after Asian crisis in *Insights into Korea* edited by The Korea Herald. Korea: The Korea Herald Herald Media, pp. 111, 112.

4 Ministry of Strategy and Finance (October 2008) *Key Issues on Korean Economy* in the Dynamic Korea.com Embassy of the Republic of Korea in the USA website, available at http://www.dynamic-korea.com/photo/Key_ Issues_on_Korean_Economy_(MOSF).pdf, accessed on 17 December 2008.

5 Ministry of Strategy and Finance (October 2008) *Corrections, Clarifications and Explanations for the October 14 Financial Times Article 'Sinking feeling'* in the Ministry of Strategy and Finance website available at www.mosf.go.kr, accessed on 17 December 2008.

6 *Ibid.*

7 *Ibid.*

8 *Ibid.*

Chapter 18

1 Fackler, M (2008). *In Japan, Financial Crisis is Just a Ripple* dated 19 September 2008 in the New York Times website, available at http://www.nytimes.com/2008/09/20/business/worldbusiness/20yen.html, accessed on 19 September 2008.

2 Yomiuri, S (2008). TROUBLE AT TOYOTA — Spreading shock waves/Impact of cutbacks hits local government coffers in *The Yomiuri Shimbun*, 20 December 2008, available at http://www.yomiuri.co.jp/dy/business/20081220TDY01301.htm, accessed on 20 September 2008.

3 *Ibid.*

Chapter 19

1 Sachs, J (2008). Action Plan to avert a global recession in *The Straits Times*. Singapore: Singapore Press Holdings, 31 October, p. A28.

2 Agence France Presse (2008). China to Boost Property Market in *The Nation*. Thailand: The Nation, 17 October 2008, p. 6B.

3 Chaitrong, W (2008). We will act if it spills over in *The Nation*. Thailand: The Nation, 17 October 2008, p. 11A.

4 Chaitrong, W (2008) We will act if it spills over in *The Nation*. Thailand: The Nation, 17 October 2008, p. 11A.

5 The Daily Telegraph (2008) China's quiet $23b splurge in UK Stock market in *Today*. Singapore: Today, 8 September, p. B2.

6 *Ibid.*

Chapter 20

1 UNIDO (2003). Lao PDR: Medium Term Strategy and Action Plan for Industrial Development Final Report, *A Comprehensive Framework Economic Initiative in Lao*

PDR. Vietiane: Government Counterpart Agency: Ministry of Industry and Handicrafts, 31 May 2003, p. xi.

2 *Ibid.*
3 *Ibid.*

Chapter 21

1 http://www.siiaonline.org/news_highlights
2 *Ibid.*

Chapter 22

1 Storey, I (2005). *China and Vietnam's Tug of War Over Laos*, in Asiamedia website, available at http://www.asiamedia.ucla.edu/article.asp?parentid=25389, accessed on 10 March 2006.
2 *Ibid.*
3 *Ibid.*
4 Bloomberg, Beijing announces $877 stimulus plan in *Today*. Singapore: Today, 10 November 2008, p. B1.
5 *Ibid.*
6 *Ibid.*
7 Tay, S (2008). Global Crisis Asian Opportunity in *The Straits Times*. Singapore: The Straits Times, 5 November 2008, p. A24.

Epilogue 1

1 Ministry of Strategy and Finance (2008) *The Korean Government's Policy Measures and Economic outlook for 2009* in the Dynamic Korea.com Embassy of the Republic of Korea in the USA, available at http://www.dynamickorea.com/news/view_news.php?main=KTD&sub=ECO&uid=200800257358&keyword=, assessed on 17 December 2008.
2 *Ibid.*

Epilogue 2

1   Goromaru, K (2008) *Fiscal 2009 budget largest ever* in the Asahi Shimbun website, available at http://www.asahi. com/english/Herald-asahi/TKY200812220062.html, assessed on 22 December 2008.

2   Ito, M (2009) Aso set to lead LDP's last stand? in *The Japan Times*, available at http://search.japantimes.co.jp/ cgi-bin/nn20090101f1.html, accessed on 1 Jan 2009.

3   D Mesler (2007) Korean economy needs new playbook for growth in *Insights into Korea*. Korea: The Korea Herald Herald Media, p. 129.

Bibliography

Books

Allen, F and D Gale (2007). *Understanding Financial Crisis*. Oxford: Oxford University Press.

Bagehot, W. *Lombard Street: A Description of the Money Market*, http://www.gutenberg.org/etext/4359

Blustein, P (2001). *Chastening: Inside the Crisis that Rocked the Global Financial System and Humbled the IMF*. New York: Public Affairs.

Braudel, F (1985). *Civilization and Capitalism Volume 2 — The Wheels of Commerce*. London: Fontana Press.

Chalmers, J (1980). *MITI and the Japanese Miracle* (California: Stanford University Press, 1980).

Communiqué of Meeting of Ministers and Governors of G-20 countries, Sao Paulo, Brazil, 8–9 November 2008.

Coyle, D (1999). *The Weightless World* (Massachusetts, MIT Press).

Dymski, G and R Pollin (1994). *New Perspectives in Monetary Macroeconomic: Explorations in the Tradition of Hyman P. Minsky*. Ann Arbor: University of Michigan Press.

Dymski, G and R Pollin (eds.) (1994). *New Perspectives in Monetary Macroeconomic: Explorations in the Tradition of Hyman P. Minsky*. Ann Arbor: University of Michigan Press.

Eichengreen, B (1999). *Toward a New International Financial Architecture: A Practical Post-Asia Agenda*, Washington, DC: Institute of International Economics.

Estabrooks, M (1995). *Electronic Technology, Corporate Strategy, and World Transformation* (USA: Quorum).

Feldstein, M (1991). The risk of economic crisis: An introduction, in Feldstein, M (ed.), *The Risk of Economic Crisis*. Chicago: University of Chicago Press.

Finer, SE (1997). *The History of Government, Volumes 2–3.* Oxford: Oxford University Press.

Hill, B (1996). *Japan Behind The Lines* (Australia: Sceptre).

Ichimura, S (1998). *Political Economy of Japan and Asian Development* (Singapore: ISEAS).

Ichimura, S (1998). *Political Economy of Japan and Asian Development.*

Keynes, JM (1936). *The General Theory of Employment, Interest and Money.* London: MacMillan.

Khor, M (2000). Globalization and the South (Malaysia: TWN).

Krugman, P (2009). *The Return of Depression Economics and the Crisis of 2008.* New York: Norton.

Lopez, RS (1976). *The Commercial Revolution of the Middle Ages, 950–1350.* Cambridge: Cambridge University Press.

Luttwak, E (1999). *Turbo Capitalism.* NY: HarpersPerennial.

March, J (1994). *A Primer on Decision Making.* New York: The Free Press.

Pollin, R and G Dymski (1994). The costs and benefits of financial instability: Big government capitalism and the Minsky Paradox.

Roberts, JM (1996). *A History of Europe.* Oxford: Helicon.

Rohwer, J (1996). *Asia Rising*, NY: Simon & Schuster.

Rutterman, PJ (1995). Financial fragility and supervision: a discussion, in Benink, HA (ed.), *Coping with Financial Fragility and Systemic Risk*, Boston: Kluwer Academic Publishers, p. 293.

Schumpeter, J (1934). *The Theory of Economic Development.* Boston: Harvard University Press.

Stiglitz, J (2004). *Roaring Nineties.* Penguin Books.

Articles/Speeches

ASEAN Secretariat (2005). "Initiative for ASEAN Integration (IAI) Work Plan for the CLMV Countries Progress Report as at 15 May 2005" in the ASEAN Secretariat website, www.aseansec.org/pdf/IAI-Article.pdf. Last accessed 7 October 2008.

Benston, GJ and Kaufman GG (1995). Is the banking and payments system fragile? *Journal of Financial Services Research*, 9, 209–240.

Fernandez, L, F Kaboub and Z Tadorova (2008). *On Democratizing Financial Turmoil: A Minskian Analysis of the Subprime Crisis*, Working Paper 548. The Levy Economics Institute of Bard College.

Fischer, S (1999). *Need for an International Lender of Last Resort.* Talk delivered to the joint luncheon of the American Economic Association and The American Finance Association, 3 Jan 1999. New York, www.imf.org/external/np/speeches/1999/010399.htm, accessed on 26 December 2008.

Kamarkar, S (2005). "India-ASEAN Cooperation in Services — An Overview" dated November 2005 in Bilaterals.org website, http://www.bilaterals.org/article.php3?id_article=6205 derived from the Indian Council for Research on International Economic Relations (ICRIER). Last accessed 1 November 2006.

Kregel, J (2008). Minsky's cushions of safety: systematic risk and the crisis in the U.S. subprime mortgage market, *Public Policy Brief*, 93, The Levy Economics Institute of Bard College.

Lim, MMH (2008). Old wine in a new bottle: subprime mortgage crisis — causes and consequences, *The Levy Economics Institute, Working Paper No: 532*, http://www.levy.org/pubs/wp_532.pdf

McKenney, JL, RO Mason and DG Copeland (1997). Bank of America: The Crest and Trough of Technological Leadership, *MIS Quarterly*, 21(3), pp. 321–353.

Ministry of Internal Affairs and Communications (MIAC) (2003). Statistics Bureau and Statistical Research and Training Institute, "Chapter 3 Economy" in the MIAC website, http://www.stat.go.jp/english/data/handbook/c03cont.htm. Last accessed 29 September 2006.

Ministry of Strategy and Finance (2008). "Corrections, Clarifications and Explanations for the October 14 Financial Times Article "Sinking feeling"" dated 14 October 2008 in the Ministry of Strategy and Finance website, www.mosf.go.kr. Last accessed on 17 December 2008.

Ministry of Strategy and Finance (2008). "Key Issues on Korean Economy" dated October 2008 in the Dynamic Korea.com Embassy of the Republic of Korea in the USA website, http://www.dynamic-korea.com/photo/Key_Issues_on_Korean_Economy_(MOSF).pdf. Last accessed 17 December 2008.

Minsky, H (1995). Financial factors in the economics of capitalism, *Journal of Financial Services Research*, 1(9), pp. 197–208.

Rosengard, J (2004). "Fiscalization of the East Asian Financial Crisis" dated March 2004 in the Kennedy School of Government website, available at ksgnotes1.harvard.edu/Research/wpaper.nsf/rwp/RWP04-012/$File/rwp04_012_rosengard.pdf.

Soesastro, H (2005). "Realizing the East Asia Vision", dated February 2005 in CSIS Working Paper Series WPE 090 (Indonesia: CSIS).

Song, SW (2001). SIIA Day 2001 Programme — The International Challenges for Singapore, Friday 2 November 2001 Session 2: The China Factor And ASEAN. Singapore: SIIA, 2001.

Sylla, R (2004). Hamilton and the Federalist financial revolution, 1789–1795, *The New York Journal of American History*, Spring 2004, pp. 32–39.

Teo, E (2001). SIIA Day 2001 Programme — The International Challenges for Singapore, Friday 2 November 2001 Session 2: The China Factor and ASEAN. Singapore: SIIA, 2001.

UNIDO (2003). "Lao PDR: Medium Term Strategy and Action Plan for Industrial Development Final Report A Comprehensive Framework to Foster Economic Initiative in Lao PDR" Vietiane: Government Counterpart Agency: Ministry of Industry and Handicrafts.

Newspaper/Magazine Articles

Agence France Presse, "China to Boost Property Market", 17 October 2008 in *The Nation* Newspaper, 2008, p. 6B

Ali, I (2007). "Dark clouds are descending over Asia's dynamism" in the *Taipei Times* website, 22 October 2007, http://www.taipeitimes.com/News/editorials/archives/204/10/22/2003207971. Last accessed 6 April 2007.

Asahi (2008). "Editorial: BOJ rate cut reasonable", 22 December, http://www.asahi.com/english/Herald-asahi/TKY200812220054.html. Last accessed 20 December 2008.

Bass, F and Beamish R (2008). AP study finds $1.6B went to bailed-out bank execs, 21 December, http://biz.yahoo.com/ap/081221/executive_bailouts.html?.v=2. Last accessed on 29 December 2008.

Bloomberg, "Beijing announces $877 stimulus plan", 10 November 2008 in *Today* (Singapore: Today), 2008, p. B1.

Bowers, S (2008). Wall Street banks in $70bn staff payout, *The Guardian*, 17 October.

Buffett warns on investment 'time bomb', *BBC News*, 4 March 2003, http://news.bbc.co.uk/2/hi/business/2817995.stm.

Carroll, C (2009). Banks and Turtles, *Financial Times*, 20 January.

Chaitrong, W (2008). "We will act if it spills over", 17 October, in *The Nation* (Thailand: The Nation), 2008, p. 11A.

Crispin, S (2001). "Thai Airways Goes It Alone" in *Far Eastern Economic Review* (HK: FEER), 26 July, p. 12.

Davis, B (2008). Nations strive for a single voice on crisis, *Asian Wall Street Journal*, 11 November.

Dombey, D, K Guha and A Ward (2008). Talks challenge club of rich countries, *Asian Wall Street Journal*, 17 November.

Don't get depressed, it's not 1929, *Newsweek*, 27 November 2008.

Drucker, P (1999). Innovate or Die, *The Economist*, 23 September.

ESCAP, "Lessons from the Asian Financial Crisis" in the UN website, http://www.un.org/Depts/rcnyo/newsletter/crisis. htm, last accessed 7 April 2007.

Fackler, M (2008). "In Japan, Financial Crisis is Just a Ripple", 19 September, in the *New York Times* website, http://www. nytimes.com/2008/09/20/business/worldbusiness/20yen. html. Last accessed 19 September 2008.

Giving credit where it is due, *The Economist*, 8 November 2008, p. 14.

Goromaru, K (2008). "Fiscal 2009 budget largest ever", 22 December, in the *Asahi Shimbun* website, http://www. asahi.com/english/Herald-asahi/TKY200812220062.html. Last accessed 22 December 2008.

Holland, T (2001). "Don't Count on the Cavalry" in FEER (HK: FEER), 26 July, p. 48, http://www.guardian.co.uk/ business/2008/oct/17/executivesalaries-banking/print. Last accessed on 29 December 2008.

Huang, J (2009). Social security crucial to higher consumption, *China Daily*, 15 January 2009, http://www.chinadaily.com. cn/cndy/2009-01/15/content_7398526.htm. Last accessed on 22 January 2009.

Ito, M (2009). "Aso set to lead LDP's last stand?", 1 January 2009 in the *Japan Times*, http://search.japantimes.co.jp/cgi-bin/nn20090101f1.html. Last accessed 1 January 2009.

Kim, SJ (2007). "Citibank CEO Warns of 2nd Asian Crisis Due to Slow Reforms", 18 May 2005 in Korea Times, http://times.hankooki.com/lpage/biz/200511/kt2005111822134411910.htm. Last accessed 6 April 2007.

Kling, A (2008). Main Street vs. Wall Street, *The American* October 3. http://www.american.com/archive/2008/october-10-08/main-street-vs.wall-street

Kwan, WK (2008). "Japan's big helping hand for families", 31 October, in *The Straits Times*, p. A11.

Lane, P (2004). Trust me, I'm a banker, *The Economist*, 17 April 2004.

Leary, A (2001). "Toothless Tiger" In Asian Business (HK: Asian Business), 7 July, p. 48.

Leow, J (2008). China seeks 'fairness', *Asian Wall Street Journal*, 7 November.

Letter to the Editor, *The Economist*, 11 October 2008, p. 20.

Manila B. (2007). "East Asia thrives a decade after crisis", 5 April, in Manila Bulletin, available at http://www.mb.com.ph/BSNS2007040691254.html. Last accessed 6 April 2007.

Mesler, D (2007). "Korean economy needs new playbook for growth" in Insights into Korea edited by The Korea Herald (Korea: The Korea Herald Herald Media), 2007, p. 129.

Not even a cat to rescue, *The Economist Online Edition*, April 20, 2006.

Ong, T (2001). "Three Themes for the Future" in *Asia-Inc* (Singapore: Asia-Inc, July).

Paulson, HM Jr (2008). Facing one challenge at a time, *International Herald Tribune*, 19 November 2008.

Sachs, J (2008). "Action Plan to avert a global recession", 31 October, in *The Straits Times* (Singapore: Singapore Press Holdings), 2008, p. A28.

Spencer, M and Juliana Lee (2007). "Korea stands firm 10 years after Asian crisis", in *Insights into Korea* edited by The Korea Herald (Korea: The Korea Herald Media), 2007, p. 111, 112.

Straits Times, "Jobless offered a roof over the head", 29 December 2008 in the Straits Times (Singapore: Straits Times), 2008, p. A7.

Takemori, S (2008). "Japan must waste no time in crisis control", 23 November, in *The Yomiuri Shimbun* website, http://www.yomiuri.co.jp/dy/business/20081123TDY08001.htm. Last accessed 23 November 2008.

Taming the beast, *The Economist*, 11 October 2008, p. 11.

Tang, SP (2007). "Asian Financial Crisis: 10 Years on", in The Straits Times, http://www.straitstimes.com/Review/Others/STIStory_134871.html. Last accessed 1 October 2007.

Tay, S (2008). "Global Crisis Asian Opportunity", 5 November, in *The Straits Times* (Singapore: Straits Times), 2008, p. A24.

The Daily Telegraph, "China's quiet $23b splurge in UK Stock market", 8 September 2008 in *Today* (Singapore: Today), 2008, p. B2.

The Daily Telegraph, "China's quiet $23b splurge in UK Stock market", 8 September 2008 in *Today* (Singapore: Today), 2008, p. B2.

The Economist (2006). "Plaza Accord" in the Economist.com website, http://www.economist.com/research/Economics/alphabetic.cfm?LETTER=P. Last accessed 29 September 2006.

The Nation, "Japan's Aso warns US Bank bail-out plan is 'insufficient'", 17 October 2008 in *The Nation* (Thailand: The Nation), 2008, p. 6B.

Trouble at Toyota — Spreading shock waves/Impact of cutbacks hits local government coffers", 20 December 2008, in *The Yomiuri Shimbun*, http://www.yomiuri.co.jp/dy/business/20081220TDY01301.htm. Last accessed 20 December 2008.

What next?, *The Economist*, 20 September 2008, pp. 13–14.

Yamamoto, T and K Nakazawa (2008). "In the Marketplace/ Electronics firms battle to lift sales", 22 December, in *The Yomiuri Shimbun*, http://www.yomiuri.co.jp/dy/business/ 20081222TDY07305.htm. Last accessed 22 December 2008.

Websites

BBC news report Summit pledge to 'restore growth', http://news.bbc.co.uk/2/hi/business/7731139.stm

CIA Factbook, "Vietnam" in the CIA World Factbook website [downloaded on 17 August 2008], available at https://www. cia.gov/library/publications/the-world-factbook/geos/ vm.html

Foreign exchange market, http://en.wikipedia.org/wiki/Foreign_ exchange_market, accessed on 21 January 2009.

Offshore bank, http://en.wikipedia.org/wiki/Offshore_banking, accessed on 21 January 2009.

Ritholtz, B (2008). Big Bailouts, Bigger Bucks, 25 November 2008, http://www.ritholtz.com/blog/2008/11/big-bailouts-bigger-bucks/

About the Authors

Dr. Michael HENG Siam-Heng is a senior research fellow at East Asian Institute, National University of Singapore. He has held academic positions in Australia, China, Malaysia, the Netherlands and Singapore. He obtained his Ph.D. in Information Systems at the Free University of Amsterdam. He previously worked as a research scientist with TNO, a Dutch applied research institute. He is an editorial board member of three international journals in the area of electronic business. He can be contacted at hsh9839@yahoo.com

Dr. LIM Tai Wei holds a joint appointment with National University of Singapore (NUS) Faculty of Arts and Social Science (FASS) and Research Fellow at the East Asian Institute, NUS. He has a law degree (LLB Hons) from University of London, First class honors degree in Japanese Studies (with Merit in Political Science) from NUS, obtained his MA in Comparative Political Economy in NUS and obtained his second MA and Ph.D. degree at the Cornell University of New York. He is the single author of the book *Oil in China: The Quest for Self-Reliance* (New York: Edwin Mellen Press, 2008) with book chapters published by City University of Hong Kong, UCSD/Cornell. His research papers have appeared in journals such as *Asian Affairs*, *North Korea Review*, *Harvard Asia Pacific Review*, *Stanford Journal of East Asian Affairs* and *Japan Focus*. He can be contacted at opiumwar@yahoo.com.

Index